THE GOSPEL UNDER SIEGE

A Study on Faith and Works

D0885642

by

Zane C. Hodges
Professor of New Testament
Dallas Seminary

REDENCIÓN VIVA

Box 141167
Dallas, Texas 75214

Additional copies of *The Gospel Under Siege* may be obtained by writing to Redención Viva, P.O. Box 141167, Dallas, TX 75214.

The cost is $4.95 per copy. Texas residents should add 5% sales tax. Add $.60 postage per book.

Second Printing, 1982
Third Printing, 1984
Fourth Printing, 1986

© 1981 by
REDENCIÓN VIVA

ISBN Number:
0-9607576-0-0

TABLE OF CONTENTS

PROLOGUE

Last night Jimmy accepted Jesus Christ as his personal Savior. This morning he is bubbling with a joy he has never experienced before.

On his way to work he meets his friend Bill. Bill has always claimed to be a Christian. He also reads a lot of books on theology. But Jimmy has never been too interested in theology up until now.

"Say, Bill," Jimmy begins, "guess what! I got saved last night. I trusted Christ as my Savior. Now I know I am going to heaven!"

"Hmmm," Bill replies, "maybe you shouldn't quite say it that way. After all, you don't really *know* that you are going to heaven."

"What do you mean?" Jimmy enquires. "The Bible says, 'Believe on the Lord Jesus Christ, and you will be saved,' and that's what I did."

Bill gives Jimmy a wise and knowing look. It is the kind of look all perceptive theologians know how to give the ignorant and the unlearned.

"But did you *really* believe? Maybe you just believed psychologically."

"What do you mean?" Jimmy is feeling a little depressed now.

"I mean," Bill continues sagely, "you can't know yet whether you have *real* saving faith."

"How can I know that?"

"By your works. You'll have to wait and see if you live a real Christian life."

Jimmy is dejected. "You mean that if I sin, I'm not a Christian after all?"

"No, I don't mean that," Bill assures him. "All Christians fail once in a while."

"But how much do they fail? I mean, how bad does it have to get before I find out I'm not saved?"

"Well, it can't get too bad for too long."

"But how bad? For how long?" Jimmy feels desperate.

"I can't tell you exactly. But a true Christian doesn't practice sin. If you find that you are practicing sin, that will show that you didn't have real saving faith to begin with."

"What if I do pretty good for several years and then things start going bad?"

"In that case, maybe you weren't saved to start with."

"Maybe? What do you mean by that?"

"I mean," Bill's tone is solemn, "you'll probably have to wait until the end of your life before you can be sure you are a true Christian. You have to persevere in good works, or your faith wasn't real."

"Do you think I can be sure before I die?"

"Maybe. Listen, Jim, I've got to rush to work. We'll talk about this some other time. Okay?"

"Yeah, okay. See you, Bill."

Bill rushes off. Jimmy is devastated. All the joy he had experienced since last night has suddenly evaporated. He is now filled with questions and doubts.

Jimmy has become a casualty in the siege of the Gospel!

CHAPTER

1

The Gospel Under Siege

" 'Unless you are circumcised according to the custom of Moses, you cannot be saved' " (Acts 15:1).

With these words the Gospel came under siege during the infancy of the Christian Church. The claim which they put forward precipitated the first theological crisis in the history of Christianity. Nothing less than the unity of the faith was at stake, and that unity was preserved only when the Jerusalem Council formally disavowed the erroneous doctrine (Acts 15:24).

But the attack has been launched again and again down through the centuries and in no age more often than in our own. The specifics may vary widely, but the format remains fundamentally the same.

"Unless you are baptized according to Biblical custom, you cannot be saved."

"Unless you persevere in good works, you cannot be saved."

"Unless you yield your life to the Lordship of Christ, you cannot be saved."

But against all such claims, whatever their form or character, the true saving Gospel stands in profound and majestic contrast: "And whoever desires, let him take the water of life freely" (Rev. 22:17).

There is no reason to doubt that the Judaizers of Acts 15 claimed to be Christians. They could scarcely have gotten a hearing in the church at Antioch if they had not made this claim. Indeed, the disavowal of their activity by the Council implies that they presented themselves as representatives of the Jerusalem church. The words "to whom we gave no such commandment" (Acts 15:24) suggest that the false teachers appealed to the authority of Jerusalem for what they taught.

Naturally this means that they acknowledged the necessity of faith in Christ. But they insisted on more than that. Salvation, they claimed, required also submission to the Mosaic law. Circumcision, of course, was the first step in that submission (cf. Gal. 5:3), and the debate at the Council focused precisely on the wider issue of obedience to the entire law (Acts 15:5; see 15:24).

In the same way, the most telling modern assaults on the integrity of the Gospel do not deny the cruciality of faith in Christ. On the contrary, they insist on it. But to faith are added other conditions, or provisos, by which the essential nature of the Gospel is radically transformed. Often, in fact, a distinction is drawn between the kind of faith which saves and the kind which does not. But the kind of faith which *does* save is always seen to be the kind that results in some form of overt obedience. By this means, the obedience itself becomes at least an implicit part of the transaction between man and God. "Saving" faith has thus been subtly redefined in terms of its fruits. In the process, the unconditional freeness of the Gospel offer is seriously, if not fatally, compromised.

Nowhere in Acts 15 is the sincerity of the Judaizers called into question. No doubt they were genuinely convinced of the truth of their claims. In all probability they had grown up in the Jewish faith. They knew also that the Mosaic law was ordained by God. It was easy for them to draw the conclusion that there could be no salvation apart from obedience to that law. But notwithstanding all this, they were still tragically wrong.

When the Council wrote that "some who went out from us have troubled you with their words, unsettling your souls" (15:24), they were not necessarily impugning the integrity of the Judaizers. But they *were* describing the effects of their doctrine. The believers at Antioch had been troubled by the words these men had spoken, and their spiritual experience had been correspondingly "unsettled."

Sincerity is no substitute for truth. It is the truth of God alone that can establish the souls of men and give them a genuine stability in holiness. "For it is a good thing," wrote the author of Hebrews, "that the heart be established by grace" (Heb. 13:9). And it is in reality the grace of God itself, in all its splendid freeness, that can truly establish God's people.

The Judaizers probably thought otherwise. Like countless others who have followed them in the professing church, they may have feared that the proclamation of a totally free salvation would lead to lawlessness and sin. To prevent this outcome, the imposition of the law may have seemed to be a moral necessity whose reasonableness was beyond dispute. But Paul and Barnabas *did* dispute it, and the Apostles and elders sided unambiguously with the proponents of grace. It was Peter himself who affirmed: "But we believe that through the grace of the Lord Jesus Christ we have been saved in the same manner as they [i.e., the Gentiles] have" (Acts 15:11, Greek).

Herein lies one of the great ironies in the history of Christian thought. The law could not guarantee "life" to men (Gal. 3:21) and was fundamentally a ministry of condemnation and guilt

(Rom. 3:19, 20; 2 Cor. 3:6–9). But despite the fact that the New Testament pronounces the law a failure in producing true holiness (see Rom. 8:3, 4), the heart of man continues to feel that its basic principle is the only workable one. According to this all too human perspective, man will not live as God desires him to live unless he is threatened with uncertainty about his eternal felicity. But as popular as this notion is, it is false. It reflects, in fact, a disastrously weak view of the power of God's truth both to create a genuinely new creature at the moment of saving faith and to transform the saved individual into the likeness of Christ. It also hopelessly misjudges the comparative power of fear and gratitude as motivations for right conduct. Beyond that, it fails to take into account the powerful inspiration furnished by objectives that are centered in eternity itself.

None of these misconceptions happens by accident. They are not only native to the soil of the human heart, but their growth is encouraged by the Enemy of souls. Paul understood, as few men have, that blindness to the Gospel is fundamentally Satanic at its core. "But even if our Gospel is veiled," he wrote, "it is veiled to those who are perishing, in whom the god of this age has blinded the minds of those who do not believe, lest the light of the gospel of the glory of Christ, who is the image of God, should shine on them" (2 Cor. 4:3, 4).

There is no mention of Satan in Acts 15. But who can doubt that the Judaizers were serving his interests and aims? Not consciously or wittingly, perhaps, but serving them nonetheless. For if the Devil wishes to blind the unregenerate world to the proclamation of the Gospel, could there be a better stratagem than to confuse the Church about its terms? If those who preach the Gospel are unclear, or even mistaken, about its contents, how shall they lead unsaved men to a knowledge of the truth?

The siege of the Gospel is not fundamentally a work of man, but a work of man's Adversary. For this purpose he can employ his own agents or he can employ well-intentioned, but misguided, Christians. The effects of the siege, wherever real inroads are made, is to dilute the Church's concept of the grace of God, to diminish her power in proclaiming the truth, and to inhibit her growth toward real spiritual maturity. It is no accident that Peter wrote: "But grow in the *grace* and knowledge of our Lord and Savior Jesus Christ" (2 Pet. 3:18; emphasis added).

It is hardly surprising, therefore, that the Apostle Paul is never more vigorous than when he is defending the purity of the Gospel. In writing to the Galatian Christians, to whom Judaizers had also come, he is utterly uncompromising. "But even if we, or an angel from heaven, preach any other gospel to you than what we have preached to you, let him be accursed. As we said before, so now I say again, if anyone preaches any other gospel to you than what you have received, let him be accursed" (Gal. 1:8, 9). The language is sharp, but it is a measure of Paul's jealousy on behalf of the true grace of God.

Of course, the Judaizers must have appealed to the Scriptures. The authority of the Mosaic law rested in the written revelation of the Old Testament. But this appeal was misguided. It misconstrued both the Old Testament itself and the new revelation which had been made through the Son of God.

In a quite similar fashion, contemporary attacks on the complete freeness of the Gospel of God's grace likewise appeal to Scripture. But invariably the appeal rests on a misconstruction of the passages in question. This is usually accompanied by the failure to face the plain meaning of the most direct statements about the way of salvation. The confusion that results is enormous. The consequences are calamitous.

In the pages that follow attention will be focused first of all upon the utter simplicity of the offer of eternal life. This offer furnishes the only grounds for real assurance of personal salvation.

Next, consideration will be given to some of the major texts that are thought to teach the necessity, or at least the inevitability, of good works in the life of a true Christian. In the process, the inconsistency of this view with the real terms of the Gospel must be faced. Additionally, along the way, some of the true motivations for Christian living must be underscored from the teaching of the New Testament.

No study of this sort could accomplish its goals without the ministry of the Holy Spirit in both writer and readers alike. The author prayerfully desires precisely this ministry to the glory of the Lord Jesus Christ.

CHAPTER

2

Can I Really Be Sure?

Few questions are more fundamental to ask than this one: Can I really be sure of my eternal salvation? Can I know that I belong to Christ and belong to Him forever?

If good works are really a condition, or an essential fruit, of salvation, the answer to this question must be: No. At least it must be "no" until the hour of one's death. For only then will it be seen—if it can even be seen then!—whether the extent of my works as well as my perseverance in them are adequate to justify the conviction that I am saved.

It does not matter how the insistence on good works is articulated. The result is inescapably the same. If works are elevated to the level of a co-condition with faith, then they are clearly indispensable to assurance. If they are only seen as the inevitable outcome of true saving faith, they become equally indispensable to assurance. For only their presence in the life can verify the authenticity of the faith from which it is claimed they must flow.

It follows, then, that when the Gospel is so presented that the necessity of good works is stressed, it becomes a gospel that no longer can honestly offer true assurance of eternal life. The individual who professes faith in Christ cannot possess, at the moment of faith, a certainty about his eternal destiny. Under some forms of contemporary theology, he cannot even be sure he has really believed! But this result is nothing less than a denial of a fundamental facet of the Biblical Gospel that was presented by our Lord Himself.

Sometimes this tragic loss of assurance is masked by the statement, "I *believe* I am a child of God." But this kind of affirmation trades on a semantic ambiguity in the English word "believe." The statement may mean, "I am *truly convinced* that I am a child of God." But it may also mean, "I *think* I am a child of God." A person who can assert no more than that he considers it probable that he is a true Christian, has not understood the New Testament offer of eternal life.

A careful consideration of the offer of salvation, as Jesus Himself presented it, will show that assurance is inherent in that offer. One forceful example of this is John 5:24, "Most assuredly, I say to you, he who hears My word and believes in Him who sent Me has everlasting life, and shall not come into judgment, but has passed from death into life." Anyone who takes this statement at face value should be able to say, "I *know* I have everlasting life. I *know* I will not come into judgment."

But if assurance arises from a simple promise like this, it can have nothing to do with works. To begin with, the statement of Jesus does not call for works. It calls only for faith. Moreover, the guarantee which He makes is relevant to the very moment of faith. "He who hears. . . believes. . . has. . . ." On the authority of Jesus, the believer can know he has eternal life at the very moment he believes God for it.

The importance of this can hardly be stressed too much. Assurance does not await the day of our death. It does not await the day when we stand before God in judgment. For here it is declared that, for the believer, there is no judgment. That is, there is no final assessment in which his destiny hangs in balance. Already he has passed out of the sphere of spiritual death and into the realm of spiritual life.

It is precisely such a verse that confronts those who insist on works with an insuperable dilemma. If works are a co-condition with faith, the Lord's failure to refer to them is inexplicable. But if works are a necessary outcome of saving faith, the problem is equally great. For in that case, one of two propositions must be true: (1) the believer also knows at the moment of faith that he will persevere in good works, or (2) the believer does not know whether he has in fact truly believed. Neither proposition can withstand scrutiny.

There are few who would wish to maintain the first proposition. Although some believe the Bible teaches that a true Christian will persevere in good works, few believe that when a man trusts Christ he can know *in advance* that he will persevere in these works. The countless warnings of the New Testament against failures of every kind ought to be sufficient to show that such a guarantee is not an integral part of Christianity. When Paul wrote to the Christians at Rome, he used these words: "For if you live according to the flesh you will die; but if you through the Spirit put to death the deeds of the body, you will live" (Rom. 8:13). In the original Greek, the form of the conditional statements in both parts of the verse is exactly the same. The level of probability is the same for both. That two possibilities are placed before the readers is as clear as words can make this.

In reference to himself, as well, the Apostle recognized the possibility of tragic failure. In 1 Corinthians 9:27 he writes: "But

I discipline my body and bring it into subjection, lest, when I have preached to others, I myself should become disqualified." In the face of a verse like this, it is not possible honestly to maintain that Paul possessed a certitude about spiritual victory. Obviously, this great servant of Christ took the spiritual dangers he faced as grim realities. He was motivated by these dangers to take care that he did not run a losing race.

In neither of the passages just mentioned, of course, is there any reason to find a threat to the believer's eternal security. A Christian who lives after the flesh is certainly in danger of death, but he is not in danger of hell. And to be disqualified in the Christian race, about which Paul is speaking in 1 Corinthians 9:24–27, is not the same as losing eternal life. More will be said of such matters in subsequent chapters. For now it is sufficient to note that an unqualified certainty about victory in Christian experience is a mirage. The New Testament cannot honestly be held to offer a certainty like this.

It is not surprising that most of those who hold that works must authenticate faith appear to adopt the second alternative. This is not always done explicitly, but it remains the only other option. If a believer cannot be certain at the time of conversion that he will live effectively for Christ, from the premise that he must do so *if* he is saved it follows that he cannot know at the time of conversion that he is truly saved. And since eternal life is offered to faith alone, then it also follows that he cannot know whether he has truly believed.

This view of things entails a psychological absurdity. At the level of everyday experience, if a man is asked whether he believes a certain fact or trusts a certain person, he can always give a definite answer. Even an answer like, "I'm not sure I trust that man," reflects a definite psychological state. What it reflects is an attitude of *dis*trust toward the individual in question. On the other hand, when someone affirms, "I trust that person," he is expressing a state of mind of which he himself is thoroughly aware. To assert that a man may profess faith in Christ without knowing whether or not he has truly trusted Christ, is to articulate an inconceivable proposition. *Of course* a man can know whether he believes in the offer of salvation or not, and the Bible everywhere takes this fact for granted. When the Philippian jailor enquired of Paul and Silas, " 'Sirs, what must I do to be saved?' " (Acts 16:30), their answer clearly offered him certainty. The words, " 'Believe on the Lord Jesus Christ, and you will be saved, you and your household' " (16:31), invite a specific, identifiable response of heart. Having made it, the jailor could know he was saved. That he did in fact know this is reflected in verse 34: "And he rejoiced, believing in God with all his household."

The seriousness of this issue must not be glossed over. An insistence on the necessity or inevitability of works fundamentally undermines assurance and postpones it, logically, until death. But the denial of assurance clashes directly with the clear intent of the Gospel proclamation as it was so often made by the Son of God Himself.

The lovely story of Jesus and the woman at the well of Sychar is a case in point. His initial offer to her was simple and direct: " 'If you knew the gift of God, and who it is who says to you, "Give Me a drink," you would have asked Him, and He would have given you living water' " (John 4:10). This is perfectly plain and carries its guarantee on its face. The woman needed only to ask, and Jesus *"would have given"* her "living water." Thus upon request, she could be *certain* she possessed eternal life. Not to be certain, was to doubt the offer itself!

It should be observed as well that the transaction of which our Lord speaks is a definitive and unrepeatable one. A few moments later He tells the woman, " 'Whoever drinks of this water [from the well] will thirst again, but whoever drinks of the water that I shall give him will never thirst' " (John 4:13, 14). The Greek phrase rendered "will never thirst" is a highly emphatic one. It might be translated, "will by no means thirst forever." According to Jesus, the need which this water meets can never reoccur. This fact clearly affirms the eternal security of the believer. For if a person could lose eternal life, he would obviously thirst again. But according to the Savior's words, that experience is an eternal impossibility.

It is hard not to be impressed with the magnificent simplicity of the transaction which Jesus proposes to this sin-laden Samaritan woman. Its very lack of complication is part of its grandeur. It is all a matter of giving and receiving and no other conditions are attached. The story constitutes a narrative exposition of the truth expressed in Revelation 22:17, "And whoever desires, let him take the water of life freely." There is no effort to extract from the woman a promise to correct her immoral life. If she wants this water, she can have it. It is free!

If the mind of man recoils from so daring an expression of divine generosity, it recoils from the Gospel itself. If it should be thought necessary to add some intrinsic guarantee that the woman would not continue her illicit liaisons—and according to Jesus, she was currently engaged in one (4:18)!—that guarantee would add to the words of our Lord Himself. The result could only be a false gospel.

It must be emphasized that there is no call here for surrender, submission, acknowledgement of Christ's Lordship, or anything else of this kind. A gift is being offered to one totally unworthy of God's favor. And to get it, the woman is required to make no spiritual commitment whatsoever. She is merely invited to ask. It is precisely this impressive fact that distinguishes the true Gospel from all its counterfeits.

Did the woman therefore simply return to her former sinful lifestyle? The Scripture does not tell us. It is not at all the point of the story! But those who think that some promise from her, expressed or implied, would have guaranteed that she did not, have an unjustified confidence in human commitments. Such an opinion would also reflect a lack of understanding about the strength of habitual sin. The bestowal of a superlatively valuable gift as an act of unconditional generosity was precisely the kind of action most likely to woo her from her former ways. It is more likely by far to have accomplished this result than any legalistic undertaking into which she might have entered.

The woman *was* grateful. Her testimony to the men proves that (4:28, 29). And Jesus had disapproved of her life (4:17, 18). There could be no more promising start than that!

But her assurance did not rest on what she might later have done. It rested instead upon the uncomplicated promise of the Son of God Himself.

Naturally it is not only in the Gospel of John that the experience of salvation is seen as an unmerited gift. Paul also saw things this way. He writes: "For by grace you have been saved through faith, and that not of yourselves; it is the gift of God, not of works, lest anyone should boast" (Eph. 2:8, 9). Here too, of course, assurance is plainly implicit in the Apostle's assertion. For Paul directly declares that the readership is saved and obviously takes it for granted that they know this. Moreover, this fact is not predicated in any way on their works but simply on God's grace and their faith. As with the woman at the well, the reception of a gift is the basic issue. The Ephesians are clearly aware of having received that gift.

Even when Paul goes on to affirm the importance of good works, the appeal is predicated on the fact that the readers are the product of God's saving activity. "For we are His workman-

ship, created in Christ Jesus for good works, which God has prepared beforehand that we should walk in them" (Eph. 2:10). Good
works are not here seen as the *evidence* that we are God's workmanship, but rather as the expected *result* of that workmanship.
Whether this result will be realized is not affirmed. But it is both
reasonable and natural to expect it to be. Since we are new creatures in Christ, that is how we should live. We should fulfill God's
purposes and walk in the works He has already prepared for us
to do.

Consequently, in Ephesians 2:8–10, good works are not the
grounds of assurance at all. On the contrary, assurance is the
grounds for good works!

How strange that so fundamental a point should be so widely
overlooked. The firmness of a relationship is the basis from which
its proper fruits can flow. Even in ordinary life this is so. Would
the relationship of a husband and wife be the same if they were
not certain whether they were married or not? Would a son have
the same response to his father if he were unsure of his paternity?
To ask these questions is to answer them. Accordingly, those who
so articulate the Gospel that the believer remains uncertain about
his final salvation actually undermine the intended effects of
God's grace. This fact compounds the seriousness of their error.

In proclaiming the Gospel of the grace of God, therefore, simplicity is at a premium. The faithful preacher or witness will
strive, with the aid of the Holy Spirit, to make the terms as lucid
as Jesus made them, or as Paul did. These standards are high, but
the infusion of works-related provisos into the proclamation must
be firmly resisted. Not to resist this is to lay ourselves open to
Satanic manipulation. It is he who wishes to blind men and to
prevent their salvation.

How simple the Gospel really is can be seen with superb clarity
in the greatest salvation passage of all. John 3:16 is perhaps more

widely familiar to people than any other verse in the Bible. And justly so. But its content is prepared for by John 3:14, 15, which declare: " 'And as Moses lifted up the serpent in the wilderness, even so must the Son of Man be lifted up, that whoever believes in Him should not perish but have eternal life.' "

Jesus is speaking, of course, to Nicodemus, a Jewish rabbi. The reference to the Old Testament furnished this man with a visual image which could illuminate the offer our Lord was making. The passage in question was Numbers 21 and its story of the fiery serpents by which the complaining Israelites were fatally bitten. Two verses in particular are worth quoting in full:

> And the Lord said unto Moses, Make thee a fiery serpent, and set it upon a pole: and it shall come to pass, that every one that is bitten, when he looketh upon it, shall live. And Moses made a serpent of brass, and put it upon a pole, and it came to pass, that if a serpent had bitten any man, when he beheld the serpent of brass, he lived (Num. 21:8, 9).

Of special interest is the Old Testament expression "shall *live*," or, "he *lived*." Its relevance to Jesus' discussion of "life" is manifest. In the ancient narrative, the afflicted Israelite was asked merely to take a look at the serpent, lifted up on the pole, and this look alone sufficed to meet his need. "When he beheld the serpent of brass, he lived"!

In the same way, Jesus means to say, He Himself will be lifted up on the cross and the one who looks to Him in faith *will live!* Could anything be more profoundly simple than that! Eternal life for one look of faith! Clearly, here too we meet the unconditional gift which may be acquired by any who desire it. "Whoever desires, let him take the water of life freely"!

It was with such a preamble that the Savior went on to utter what must surely be the most fruitful declaration ever made in the history of man. " 'For God so loved the world that He gave His only begotten Son, that whoever believes in Him should not perish but have everlasting life' " (John 3:16). The number of people who have found the assurance of salvation in these words defies all computation.

And assurance is precisely what one *should* find in them. There is no mention of works. Faith alone is the one condition upon which a man may acquire everlasting life. Moreover, this secures him from perishing. Indeed, if anyone who ever trusted Jesus for eternal life subsequently perished, the verse would be false. "Whoever believes" is as broad as it can possibly be and is wholly unqualified by any other stipulation. Those who wish to qualify it, in fact deny it.

There is no question here of "this kind of faith" versus "that kind of faith," or "a faith which leads to this rather than to that." The issue is simply faith in the divine offer. Will a man *look* to the Crucified One for eternal life, or will he not? The man who does, *lives!* In this way, the Gospel confronts, and refutes, all its contemporary distortions.

Yes, I really *can* be sure!

CHAPTER

3

What Is A Dead Faith?

"Faith without works is dead." So spoke James in the second chapter of his epistle. His assertion has been appealed to many times to support the view that works are indispensable to a man's eternal salvation.

Sometimes, of course, it is frankly claimed that unless faith is followed by good works, the believer forfeits eternal life. At other times, a more subtle approach is taken. If a professing Christian does not manifest good works, he was never a true believer to begin with. Whatever James is saying, however, it can be neither of these ideas.

The second view, in particular, is so untenable that if it were not maintained by obviously sincere men, it might be called dishonest. According to this view, a dead faith cannot save. Therefore, if a man lacks the crucial evidence of good works, it shows that this is all he has ever possessed—a dead faith.

This flies directly into the face of the text. In James 2:26 the writer affirms, "For as the body without the spirit is dead, so faith without works is dead also." No one who encountered a dead body whose vitalizing spirit had departed, would ever conclude that the body had never been alive. Quite the contrary. The presence of a corpse is the clearest proof of a *loss* of life. If we allow this illustration to speak for itself, then the presence of a dead faith shows that this faith was once alive.

Nor is there *anything at all* in the entire passage to support some other inference. As elsewhere in the epistle, it is Christian brothers who are addressed (2:14; cf. 1:2, 16, 19; 2:1, 5; 3:1, 10, 12; etc.). There is absolutely nothing to suggest James believed that if a man's faith is pronounced dead, it must therefore always have been dead. This deduction is not the product of exegesis at all. It is rather a desperate expedient designed to salvage some form of harmony between James and the doctrine of Paul. But by distorting the true meaning of the text, it has given rise to immense confusion which has had an adverse impact on men's comprehension of the Gospel of God's saving grace.

One must observe at the very outset that, like all the inspired writers, James believed that eternal life was the gracious gift of God. This is made plain in a splendid passage in his first chapter:

Every good gift and every perfect gift is from above, and comes down from the Father of lights, with whom there is no variation or shadow of turning. Of His own will He brought us forth by the word of truth, that we might be a kind of firstfruits of His creatures (Jam. 1:17, 18).

Anyone who is familiar with the words of Jesus, as James certainly was, will not mistake the resonances of a statement like this. New birth is a sovereign act of God. It is one of His good and perfect gifts which comes down from above.

In fact, in the expression "from above," James employs exactly the same word that Jesus used when He told Nicodemus, "You must be born *again*" (John 3:7). The Greek term in question is *anōthen* and means both "again" and "from above." Its selection by our Lord for His discourse with Nicodemus was no doubt deliberate. The supernatural birth which He was describing is both a *rebirth* and a *birth from above*. The play on words which this involves is an effective one.

One notices in James' affirmation about our rebirth the strong emphasis on the sovereign volition of God. "Of His own will He brought us forth. . ." James insists. This perspective is reminiscent of the Pauline statement found in 2 Corinthians 4:6, "For it is the God who commanded light to shine out of darkness who has shone in our hearts to give the light of the knowledge of the glory of God in the face of Jesus Christ." Here, too, the sovereign act of God is stressed.

Neither Paul nor James intends by such words to deny the necessity of faith. But faith, as we have perceived it in the simple, direct statements of the Bible about the saving transaction, is nothing more than a response to a divine initiative. It is the means by which the gift of life is received. Since this is so, it is altogether proper that God Himself should be viewed as the Sovereign Actor at the moment of conversion. It is He who decides to regenerate. We simply open ourselves to that action with the receptivity of a believing heart.

There is thus no reason to doubt that James and Paul were in fundamental harmony about the way eternal life is received. For both of them it is the gift of God, graciously and sovereignly bestowed. It is remarkable, however, that it is precisely when we take this unity of perspective for granted, that we can really understand the meaning of James' instruction about works.

The place to start is where James starts. In James 2:14, his famous discussion is opened with the words, "What does it profit, my brethren, if someone says he has faith but does not have works? Faith cannot save him, can it?" The translation just given is based on the original Greek and is crucial to correct interpretation. The form of the question which James asks in the last part of the verse is one which implies a negative response. The expected answer, from James' point of view, would be: "No, faith cannot save him." Of course, anyone who held that faith and works were both conditions for reaching heaven would have no problem with a question like this. For them, it would simply assert that faith by itself was not enough. It should be squarely faced, in fact, that this is precisely what James says in verse 17. "Thus also faith by itself, if it does not have works, is dead."

But the problem comes in attempting to synthesize this kind of statement with the Apostle Paul's unambiguous denial that works are a condition for salvation. For Paul, the intrusion of works would be a denial of grace. He is emphatic on this point: "And if by grace, then it is no longer of works; otherwise grace is no longer grace. But if it is of works, then it is no longer grace; otherwise work is no longer work" (Rom. 11:6). It is hard to quarrel with this point of view! In fact it is impossible to do so. Paul's point is that once works are made a condition for attaining some goal, that goal can no longer be said to be attained by grace.

But in James 2, James plainly makes works a *condition* for salvation. The failure to admit this is the chief source of the problems supposedly arising from this passage for most evangelicals. We ought to start by admitting it.

But instead of this being admitted, it has often been evaded. This is frequently done by trying to translate the question, "Can faith save him?" (2:14), by "Can that [or, such] faith save him?" But the introduction of words like "that" or "such" as qualifiers for "faith" is, in the last analysis, an evasion of the text. The Greek does not at all validate this sort of translation expedient.

The justification for the renderings "such faith" or "that faith" is usually sought in the presence of the Greek definite article with the word "faith." But in this very passage, the definite article also occurs with "faith" in verses 17, 18, 20, 22 and 26. (In verse 22, the reference is to Abraham's faith!) In none of these places are the words "such" or "that" proposed as natural translations. In fact, as is well known, the Greek language often employed the definite article with abstract nouns where English cannot do so. The attempt to single out 2:14 for specialized treatment carries its own refutation on its face. James' point is quite simple: faith alone cannot save.

But what are we left with? A contradiction between James and Paul? This is what many have candidly thought, and it is easy to see why. If James and Paul are talking about the same thing, they *do* contradict each other. But are they talking about the same thing?

In the opening chapter of the epistle, shortly after declaring his readers to be the offspring of God's regenerating activity (1:18), James writes:

> Therefore lay aside all filthiness and overflow of wickedness, and receive with meekness the implanted word, which is able to save your souls. But be doers of the word, and not hearers only, deceiving yourselves (Jam. 1:21, 22).

That this passage is analogous to 2:14 is easy to see. Here too James is affirming the necessity of *doing* something, and he clearly means that only if his readers *do* God's Word will it be able to "save their souls."

At first glance, this seems only to repeat the problem already encountered. But in fact it offers us the solution. The reason we do not see it immediately is due to the fact that we are English speakers with a long history of theological indoctrination. To us, the expression "save your souls" can scarcely mean anything else than "to be delivered from hell."

But this is the meaning *least likely* to occur to a Greek reader of the same text. The fact is that the expression "to save the soul" represents a Greek phrase whose most common meaning in English would be "to save the life." In the New Testament it occurs in this sense in the parallel passages, Mark 3:4 and Luke 6:9 (see also Luke 9:56). Among the numerous places where it is used with this meaning in the Greek translation of the Old Testament, the following references would be especially clear to the English reader: Genesis 19:17 and 32:30; 1 Samuel 19:11; and Jeremiah 48:6. Perhaps even more to the point, the phrase occurs again in James 5:20 and here the words "from death" are explicitly added.

By contrast, the expression is never found in any New Testament text which describes the conversion experience!

The natural sense of the Greek phrase (i.e., "to save your lives") fits perfectly into the larger context of James 1. Earlier James was discussing the consequences of sin. He has said, "Then, when desire has conceived, it gives birth to sin; and sin, when it is full-grown, brings forth death" (1:15). It is easy to see how obedience to the Word of God can "save the life" from the death-dealing outcome of sin. There is even an echo of the Pauline truth, "If you live according to the flesh you will die" (Rom. 8:13).

With this construction of James 1:21, the statement of 5:19, 20 agrees completely. That statement, too, is addressed to Christians:

> Brethren, if anyone among you should wander from the truth, and someone turns him back, let him know that he who turns a sinner from the error of his way will save a soul from death and cover a multitude of sins.

On this attractive note of mutual spiritual concern among the brethren, James closes his letter. But in doing so, he manages to emphasize once again that sin can lead to death.

It has often been observed that the Epistle of James is, of all the New Testament writings, the one which most clearly reflects the wisdom literature of the Old Testament. The theme of death as the consequence of sin is an extremely frequent one in the book of Proverbs. A few illustrative texts may be mentioned:

The fear of the Lord prolongeth days: but the years of the wicked shall be shortened (Pro. 10:27).

As righteousness tendeth to life: so he that pursueth evil pursueth it to his own death (Pro. 11:19).

In the way of righteousness is life; and in the pathway thereof there is no death (Pro. 12:28).

The law of the wise is a fountain of life, to depart from the snares of death (Pro. 13:14).

He that keepeth the commandment keepeth his own soul [i.e., his life!]; but he that despiseth his ways shall die (Pro. 19:16).

It should be evident that this is the Old Testament concept which furnishes the background for James' thought. A recognition of this fact clarifies a great deal.

It is best to regard James 1:21–2:26 as a single large unit in the argument of the epistle. James 1:21 sets the theme. The readers, who are born-again Christians (1:18), need to lay wickedness aside and receive the Word of God as the agent capable of saving their lives. But they must understand (1:22–25) that this will only occur if they are *doers* of the Word and not mere hearers. To be a mere hearer is to commit the folly of looking into the divine mirror of truth and forgetting what it tells us about ourselves. Only the man who is a *"doer of work"* (1:25) can expect God's blessing on his life.

There follows in 1:26–2:13 some specific information about what a "doer of work" actually does. He controls his tongue, is charitable to the needy and keeps aloof from worldly sin (1:26–27). Moreover, he rejects the spirit of partiality and favoritism which is so common in the world (2:1–13). That spirit is wholly inconsistent with one's faith in the Lord of Glory (2:1). In its place should be a true obedience to "the royal law according to the Scripture, 'You shall love your neighbor as yourself' " (2:8). In fact love and its handmaiden, mercy, are standards by which the lives of believers will be assessed at the Judgment Seat of Christ. They should therefore "so speak and so do as those who will be judged by the law of liberty" (2:12). The reference back to 1:25 is patent.

In referring to judgment, of course, James does not contradict the assertion of John 5:24 that the believer does not come into judgment. There is *no* judgment for the regenerate person if by that term is meant a weighing of his merits in terms of heaven or hell. But the New Testament does teach an assessment of the believer's earthly experience in connection with rewards, or the loss of these. (See 1 Cor. 3:12–15; 2 Cor. 5:10.) More will be said of this in a later chapter.

James 2:14–26 is the final sub-section of the larger unit, 1:21–2:26. At 2:14 James returns to the thought expressed in 1:21 about "saving the life." Since he has insisted that this is only possible when one is actually a *"doer of work"*[!], he wishes now to oppose the idea that faith can substitute for obedience and accomplish the same saving result he had mentioned to begin with. Can the fact that a man holds correct beliefs and is orthodox preserve him from the deadly consequences of sin? Of course not! The very thought is absurd. That is like giving your best wishes to a destitute brother or sister when what they really need is food and clothing (2:15–16). It is utterly fruitless!

As a matter of fact, this kind of callous conduct on the part of one Christian toward another is precisely what James has been warning against (cf. 1:27; 2:2–6)! It superbly illustrates his point.

This leads James to say, "Thus also faith by itself, if it does not have works, is dead" (2:17). It has not usually been considered too deeply why James chose the term "dead" to describe a faith that is not working. But the moment we relate this to the controlling theme of "saving the life," everything becomes plain. The issue that concerns James is an issue of life or death. (He is *not* discussing salvation from hell!) The truth which he has in mind is that of Proverbs: "Righteousness tendeth to life . . . he that pursueth evil pursueth it to his own death." Can a *dead* faith save the Christian from *death?* The question answers itself. The choice of the adjective "dead" is perfectly suited to James' argument.

In 2:18–19 James introduces the words of an imagined objector. The entirety of these verses belong to the objector. The response only begins in verse 20 as is shown by the words, "But do you want to know, O foolish man. . . ." The format James employs here was a familiar one from the Greek diatribe, a learned and argumentative form of ancient literature. Elsewhere in the New Testament, this format appears in 1 Corinthians 15:35, 36.

Since the assertions in verse 19 about the belief of men and demons are the words of the objector—not of James!—their frequent use to make a theological point is totally misguided. But what does the objection mean? Since most Greek manuscripts read the word "by" in place of the familiar word "without" in verse 18, the objector's statement may be given as follows:

But someone will say:
"You have faith and I have works. Show me your faith by your works, and I will show you, from my works, my faith. You believe that there is one God; you do well. The demons also believe, and tremble" (Jam. 2:18, 19, Greek).

The argument which these words express appears to be a reductio ad absurdum (a reduction to absurdity). It is absurd, says the objector, to see an intimate connection between faith and works. You can no more take your faith and show me your works, than

I can take my works and show you my faith. Men and demons may even believe the same truth (that there is one God), but their faith has no correlation to what they do. Such a conviction may move a man to "do well," but it never moves the demons to "do well." All they can do is tremble.

No doubt James and his readers had heard this argument before. It was precisely the kind of defensive approach a man might take when his orthodoxy was not supported by good deeds. "Faith and works are not really related to each other in the way you say they are, James. So don't impugn the quality of my faith because I don't do such and such a thing."

James' reply (2:20) may be paraphrased: "What a senseless argument! How foolish you are to make it! I still say that without works your faith is dead. Would you like to know why?"

Verses 21–23 are James' direct rebuttal of the professed objection. This is made clear in the Greek text by the singular form of "do you see" in verse 22. Only with the "you see" of verse 24 does James return to the plural and to his readers as a whole.

In refuting the objection he has cited, James selects the most prestigious name in the annals of Jewish history, the patriarch Abraham. He selects also his most honored act of obedience to God, the offering of his own son Isaac. Since in Christian circles it was well known that Abraham was justified by faith, James now adds a highly original touch. He was also justified by works!

Earlier in this discussion it was suggested that we can best understand James' point of view by granting his harmony with Paul. That is extremely pertinent here. James does not wish to deny that Abraham, or anyone else, could be justified by faith alone. He merely wishes to assert that there is also another justification, and it is by works. There is, of course, no such thing as a single justification by faith *plus* works. Nothing James says suggests that. Rather, there are two kinds of justification.

This point is confirmed by a careful reading of the Greek text of verse 24. When he returns to his readers generally, James says, "You see then that a man is justified by works, and not only [justified] by faith." The key to this understanding is the Greek adverb "only," which does not modify simply the word "faith" but the whole idea of the second clause. James is saying: Justification by faith is not the *only* kind of justification there is. There is also the kind which is by works.

Somewhat surprisingly, to most people, the Apostle Paul tacitly agrees with this. Writing at what was no doubt a later time than James, Paul states in Romans 4:2, "For if Abraham was justified by works, he has something of which to boast, but not before God." The form of the conditional statement is one which does not, by itself, deny the truth of the point under consideration. The phrase, "but not before God," strongly suggests that the Apostle can conceive of a sense in which the condition could be true. But, he insists, that is not the way men are justified before God. That is, it does not establish their legal standing before Him.

In responding, therefore, to the kind of person who tried to divorce faith and works in Christian experience, James strikes upon a skillful approach. "Wait a moment, you foolish man," he is saying, "you make much of justification by faith, but can't you see how Abraham was also justified by works when he offered his son Isaac to God?" (2:21) "Is it not obvious how his faith was cooperating with his works and, in fact, by works his faith was made mature?" (2:22). "In this way, too, the full significance of the Scripture about his justification by faith was brought to light, for now he could be called the friend of God" (2:23).

The content of this passage is rich indeed. It is a pity that it has been so widely misunderstood. The faith which justifies—James never denies that it *does* justify!—can have an active and vital role in the life of the obedient believer. As with Abraham, it can be the dynamic for superb acts of obedience. In the process, faith itself can be "perfected." The Greek word suggests development and maturation. Faith is thus nourished and strengthened by works.

It would hardly be possible to find a better illustration of James' point anywhere in the Bible. The faith by which Abraham was justified was implicitly faith in a God of resurrection. Referring to the occasion when that faith was first exercised, Paul wrote:

> And not being weak in faith, he did not consider his own body, already dead (since he was about a hundred years old), and the deadness of Sarah's womb. He did not waver at the promise of God through unbelief, but was strengthened in faith, giving glory to God, and being fully convinced that what He had promised He was also able to perform (Rom. 4:19–21).

Abraham had confidence that the God he believed in could overcome the "deadness" of his own body and of Sarah's womb. But it was only through the testing with Isaac that this faith becomes an explicit conviction that God could literally raise a person from the dead to fulfill His oath. Accordingly, the author of Hebrews declares:

> By faith Abraham, when he was tested, offered up Isaac, and he who had received the promises offered up his only begotten son, of whom it was said, "In Isaac your seed shall be called," accounting that God was able to raise him up, even from the dead, from which he also received him in a figurative sense" (Heb. 11:17–19).

Thus was the faith of Abraham strengthened and matured by works! From a conviction that God could overcome a metaphorical "deadness" exhibited by his own body, he moved to the assurance that, if necessary, God could actually resurrect his son's body from a deadness which would be all too painfully literal.

In the process of carrying out the divine command to sacrifice his beloved boy, his faith grew and reached new heights of explicitness!

In this way, too, the Scripture that cited his original justification "was fulfilled." That text (Gen. 15:6) was not a prophecy, of course. But its implications were richly developed and exposed by the subsequent record of Abraham's obedience. Abraham's works "filled it full" of meaning, so to speak, by showing the extent to which that faith could develop and undergird a life of obedience. Simple and uncomplicated though it was at first, Abraham's justifying faith had potential ramifications which only his works, built on it, could disclose.

And now he could be called "the friend of God," not only by God Himself but also by men (cf. Isa. 41:8; 2 Chron. 20:7). This is in fact the name by which Abraham has been known down through the centuries in many lands and by at least three religions! Had he not obeyed God in the greatest test of his life, he would still have been justified by the faith he exercised in Genesis 15:6. But by allowing that faith to *be alive* in his works, he attained an enviable title among men. In this way, he was also justified by works!

When a man is justified by faith he finds an unqualified acceptance before God. As Paul puts it, such a man is one "to whom God imputes righteousness without works" (Rom. 4:6). But only God can see this spiritual transaction. When, however, a man is justified by works he achieves an intimacy with God that is manifest to men. He can then be called "the friend of God," even as Jesus said, "You are My friends if you do whatever I command you" (John 15:14).

Leaving the imagined objector behind, James returns in verses 24–26 to address the readership directly. Rahab furnishes him with his final Biblical example of justification by works. "Likewise," he writes, "was not Rahab the harlot also justified by works. . .?" (2:25).

It should be carefully observed that he does *not* say, "Was not Rahab justified by faith *and* works"! As already mentioned, such a conception is quite foreign to James. He is talking about exactly what he says he is talking about: justification by works!

Rahab, however, is superbly suited to tie the strands of his thought together. The passage had begun, as we have seen, with an allusion to his theme of "saving the life" (2:14; 1:21). Not surprisingly, therefore, Rahab is selected as a striking example of a person whose physical life was "saved" precisely because she had works.

With James' words the statement of the writer of Hebrews can be profitably compared. In 11:31, he writes of her:

> **By faith the harlot Rahab did not perish with those who did not believe, when she had received the spies with peace.**

It will be noted that the author of Hebrews points to her faith and lays the stress on the fact that she "received" the spies. James, on the other hand, points also to the fact that "she sent them out another way." This has considerable significance for his argument.

Although Rahab's faith began to operate the moment she "received the messengers," she could not be really justified by works until she had "sent them out another way." The reason for this is obvious when the story in Joshua 2 is carefully considered. Up until the last moment, she could still have betrayed the spies. Had she so desired, she could have sent their pursuers after them. That the spies had lingering doubts about her loyalty is suggested by their words in Joshua 2:20, "And if thou utter this our business, then we will be quit of thine oath. . . ." But the spies' successful escape demonstrated that Rahab was truly the "friend of God" because she was also *their* friend. In this way, Rahab was justified by works!

And in the process, she saved her own life and her family's! Her faith, therefore, was very much *alive* because it was an active, working faith. Though she was a harlot—and both inspired writers remind us that she was—her living faith triumphed over the natural consequences of her sin. While all the inhabitants of Jericho perished under the divine judgment which Israel executed, she *lived* because her faith *lived!*

James therefore wishes his readers to know that works are in fact the vitalizing "spirit" which keeps one's faith alive in the same way that the human spirit keeps the human body alive (2:26). Whenever a Christian ceases to act on his faith, that faith atrophies and becomes little more than a creedal corpse. "Dead orthodoxy" is a danger that has always confronted Christian people and they do well to take heed to this danger. But the antidote is a simple one: faith remains vital and alive as long as it is being translated into real works of living obedience.

Does James then contradict Paul's doctrine of free grace, or John's insistence on faith as the single condition for eternal life? Far from it. But neither does he offer support to the widespread notion that a "dead faith" cannot exist in the life of a Christian. Ironically, that is exactly what he is warning against. Thus the misconstruction of his words has not only bred unnecessary confusion about the terms for eternal life, but it has also deprived the Church of a much needed and salutary warning.

The dangers of a dying faith are real. But they do not include hell, and nothing James writes suggests this. Nevertheless, sin remains a deadly nemesis to Christian experience which can end our physical lives themselves. To that, the wisdom of the Old Testament adds its witness to the warnings of James. And if a man is to be saved from *such* a consequence, he *must* have works!

CHAPTER

4

The Cost Of Discipleship

One fact which the Lord Jesus Christ made completely clear was that discipleship entailed a costly commitment. On that point His words left no doubt.

A classic expression of this truth is found in Luke 14:26, 27. There the Savior declares: " 'If anyone comes to Me and does not hate his father and mother, wife and children, brothers and sisters, yes, and his own life also, he cannot be My disciple. And whoever does not bear his cross and come after Me cannot be My disciple.' " Later, in the same context (14:33), He says, " 'So likewise, whoever of you does not forsake all that he has, he cannot be My disciple.' "

It is part of the contemporary siege of the Gospel that such words are today often taken as expressing virtual conditions for eternal salvation. The word "virtual" is deliberately chosen. By some it would be affirmed that those who do not fulfill the terms of discipleship will not go to heaven. Yet at the same time they might insist on the Pauline truth that a man is saved by grace through faith and apart from works. The transparent inconsistency of this is glaring.

By no stretch of the imagination can the words of Jesus in Luke 14 be treated as portraying the "inevitable result" of regeneration. There is absolutely nothing in the passage to suggest that. On the contrary, the obvious purpose of the Lord's statements is to warn against the very real danger of failure.

The well-known image of the man and the uncompleted tower serves to highlight this aspect of the passage. The words with which he is mocked carry a pointed message: "This man began to build and was not able to finish." In the same way, the metaphor of the king who sues for peace carries a similar warning.

If the claim is advanced that no real Christian is subject to such failure, that claim amounts to little more than an evasion of the warning itself. Certainly there is nothing in the Biblical text to support this point of view. To invoke it is to beg the question.

It is high time for candor in the evangelical church. Luke 14, to name only this text, clearly states the *conditions* for discipleship. If to be a Christian is to be a disciple, then Luke 14 gives also the *conditions* for being a Christian. Another way of saying this is that if one does not meet the standards of discipleship he is not, and cannot claim to be, a true Christian. But "standards" which must be met to assure a given outcome are obviously "requirements" by which that outcome is conditioned. To say less than this is to be less than candid.

The issue can be simply put. Can a man who trusts Christ for eternal life but fails to "hate" his father and mother go to heaven? If the answer to this is "no," then it is perfectly clear that "hating" one's father and mother is a *condition* for ultimate felicity. No amount of theological re-articulation can conceal this result. But in the process, the terms of the Biblical Gospel have been radically transformed. Heaven cannot be reached except by the most strenuous self-denial and loyalty to Christ. A salvation by faith plus works is thereby affirmed.

How serious this is can hardly be overstated. Those who so express their conception of the Gospel of Christ, must necessarily feel restless and uncomfortable in the presence of our Lord's free and unencumbered offer to the sinful woman of Sychar. Had she been told the stringent demands of Luke 14, she could scarcely have imagined that she was being offered a *gift!* For that matter, who could?

It is an interpretative mistake of the first magnitude to confuse the terms of discipleship with the offer of eternal life as a free gift. "And whoever desires, let him take the water of life freely" (Rev. 22:17), is clearly an unconditional benefaction. "If any one comes to me and does not . . . he cannot be My disciple" clearly expresses a relationship which is fully conditional. Not to recognize this simple distinction is to invite confusion and error at the most fundamental level.

The distinction in question is openly recognized in the Gospel of John. In John 8:30 we are told, "As He spoke these words, many believed in Him." In the original Greek, the words "believed in Him" represent a special construction which is almost (though not quite) unique to the Fourth Gospel. This construction involves the use of a Greek preposition (*eis*) after the verb for "believe" and, so far at least, it has not been found in secular Greek. Among the instances of its use in John's Gospel may be mentioned the following: 1:12; 2:11; 3:15, 16, 17, 18, 36; 6:29, 35, 40, 47; 7:38, 39; 9:35, 36; 10:42; 11:25, 26, 45; and 12:44, 46.

Even a cursory examination of these texts shows that this specialized expression is John's standard way of describing the act of saving faith by which eternal life is obtained. To deny this in John 8:30 would be to go directly counter to the well-established usage of the author. Yet precisely to these individuals who had exercised saving faith, Jesus adds:

> "If you continue in My word, then you are My disciples
> indeed. And you shall know the truth, and the truth shall
> make you free" (8:31, 32).

On the authority of Jesus Himself it can be said that the believers of John 8:30 received eternal life in response to their faith. It was He who had affirmed, "Most assuredly, I say to you, he who believes in Me has everlasting life" (John 6:47). But to these who now had that life, Jesus set forth a *conditional* relationship: "*if* you continue in My word, then you are My disciples indeed." The Greek conditional clause is one that is cast in a hypothetical form and assumes nothing about the fulfillment of the condition itself.

Plainly we have here, as also in Luke 14, a relationship which is contingent on the individual's continuing commitment to the discipleship experience. Should this commitment fail, he would become like the man who "began to build and was not able to finish." But this reality should not be confused with a man's permanent possession of the gift of eternal life. That gift, like all God's gifts, is irrevocable (Rom. 11:29) and the one who acquires it can never hunger or thirst for it again (John 6:35). Moreover, the Lord Jesus Christ has never yet lost anyone who trusted Him for it (John 6:37–40).

Notwithstanding what has just been said, it has actually been argued that the individuals of John 8:30 exercised a faith that was not regenerating. Appeal is sometimes made to the Greek construction of verse 31 in the phrase "the Jews who believed Him." Here it is said that John uses an expression without the preposition (that is, without the *eis* found in verse 30) and that this helps signal the inadequacy of the faith which these Jews had.

This argument is groundless. John knows nothing about a faith in Christ that is not saving. The construction found in verse 31 appears also in John 5:24 where no one would regard it as expressing faulty belief. It is equally obvious that the individuals of verse 31 are the same as those of verse 30 of whom John employs his specialized terminology. The effort to distinguish different *kinds* of faith, both here and elsewhere, is entirely futile. (John 2:23 and 12:42 are sometimes adduced, but on question-begging grounds.)

It has also been claimed, however, that the believing Jews of verses 30, 31 are the speakers in verses 33, 39 and 41. It is then pointed out that in verse 44 Jesus tells them, "You are of your father the devil, and the desires of your father you want to do." Along with the whole tenor of verses 33–47—and especially the statements of verses 39, 40 and 42—this is seen as a clear indication that the faith described in 8:30 was not regenerating faith. But this argument involves a misassessment of the whole context in which verses 8:30–32 are placed.

John 8:13–59 is clearly a controversy section which has its setting in the Jewish Temple (8:20). Jesus' interlocutors and opponents throughout the section are his general audience in the Temple treasury. They are described as Pharisees (8:13), as Jews (8:22, 48, 52 and 57) and more simply as "they" (8:19, 25, 27, 33, 39, 41, 59). John does not expect us to construe the "they" of verse 33 any differently than we do the same word in verses 19, 25 and 27. He intends the larger audience. Verses 30–31a (about those who believe in Him) are a kind of "aside" to the reader to explain the background and purpose of Jesus' statement in verses 31b–32 (about continuing in His Word). The reader is in this way allowed to perceive the reason why Jesus' words are misunderstood and how they serve to intensify the controversy that is already raging.

This technique is Johannine to the core. Throughout the Fourth Gospel, the words of Jesus are frequently misconstrued (cf. 3:4; 4:11, 12; 6:34; 7:35; 8:22; etc.). Where necessary, John offers the readers the relevant clue to their actual meaning (cf. 2:19–22; 11:11–13). There is thus no reason at all to suppose that in affirming that "many believed in Him" (8:30) he means anything different than he does with nearly identical statements in 10:42 and 11:45. The effort to see the "believers" of 8:30, 31 as belonging to some special category (like an "unregenerate believer"!) is without foundation and is totally misguided.

John 8:30–32 can stand therefore as a significant contribution to our understanding of the difference between the terms of discipleship and the condition for receiving eternal life. The latter here, as everywhere in the Fourth Gospel, is the result of faith. But discipleship depends upon the believer's continuance in the Word of Christ. This is plain enough and should occasion no confusion at all.

Of course, the Greek word for "disciple" meant simply a "pupil" or a "learner." Thus a disciple was one who was "in school"—that is, he was under the guidance and instruction of a teacher. By no means all of these had classrooms or lecture halls, as Tyrannus of Ephesus evidently did (Acts 19:9). The idea of a peripatetic, or travelling, teacher was far from unusual in the ancient Greco-Roman world. Hence, there is nothing strange about the thought of leaving home and family to follow such a teacher around and to benefit from his tutelage.

The cultural gap between ourselves and the first century has probably contributed somewhat to the modern confusion about the concept of discipleship. No doubt close attention to the Scriptures could have spared us from that. But it is important to see things like this from the perspective of their historical setting. It would surprise no one in the first century to be told that someone who had left home to follow a travelling teacher might be tempted to "drop out" and return to his loved ones. Hence continuance in the Word of Christ and a devotion to Him even above the family itself are precisely the natural conditions for the kind of relationship which discipleship describes. By contrast, regeneration points to a family relationship in which God becomes the Father of the one who trusts His Son. Such relationships on earth are permanent. The divine family is no exception.

It is not surprising that in the book of Acts the word "disciple" becomes a standard way of describing those who became a part of the visible church. The "school" in which they now received their instruction was the church itself. It was there that the doctrine of the Apostles brought them into vital contact with all that Jesus Himself had taught these original disciples. In this way the first disciples reproduced themselves by making other disciples. The steps involved in this were twofold as Matthew 28:19, 20 disclose:

> "Go therefore and make disciples of all the nations, **baptizing** them in the name of the Father and of the Son and of the Holy Spirit, **teaching** them to observe all things whatever I have commanded you; and behold, I am with you always, even to the end of the age" [emphasis added].

The process of disciple-making involves, therefore, an initiation (baptizing) followed by indoctrination (teaching). Both steps were begun promptly on the first day of the Church's history immediately after the conversion of three thousand souls (Acts 2:41, 42)!

In passing it may be noted that from the beginning baptism was associated with the making of disciples. John notes that "the Pharisees had heard that Jesus made and baptized more disciples than John (though Jesus Himself did not baptize, but His disciples)" (John 4:1, 2). Baptism may thus be properly seen as the first concrete step which a disciple takes in obedience to Christ.

It is of considerable interest that the word used by our Lord in John 8:31 to describe the responsibility of a disciple is an important one in the Fourth Gospel. The word "continue" is exactly the same word that is translated "abide" in John 15:1–7 where it is the crucial term in the metaphor about the vine and its branches. Of course, the same word can be used of the mutually shared life of the believer and Christ (John 6:56) as well as of a purely physical dwelling (= "staying," John 1:38, 39). But in John 15 its role in the metaphor is evidently to describe the discipleship experience.

This observation can be directly supported from the text. The discussion of the vine and branches is concluded in 15:8 with the words: "By this My Father is glorified, that you bear much fruit; *so you will be My disciples*" (emphasis added). Recognition that this famous passage pertains to discipleship effectually dissolves the problems which have been often associated with it.

As has been already observed, discipleship is a conditional relationship that can be interrupted or terminated after it has begun. This is obviously also true of the vine-branch relationship described in John 15. It is the responsibility of Jesus' disciples (to whom these words are spoken) to "abide" in Him (15:4). When this condition is fulfilled, there is fruitfulness (15:5) and answered prayer (15:7). (These two results may in fact be a way of saying the same thing—see 15:16.) If the condition is *not* fulfilled, tragic consequences ensue (15:6).

The consequences that follow when a disciple fails to abide in Christ are fully comprehensible in terms of this kind of relationship. First, there is the loss of the relationship itself: "he is cast out as a branch." Next, there is the loss of the spiritual vitality associated with that relationship: "and is withered." Finally, there is chastening: "they gather them and throw them into the fire, and they are burned."

It is entirely unnecessary, of course, to associate the "fire" of John 15:6 with the literal fires of hell. After all, the entire passage involves a figure of speech. The "vine" is not a literal vine, the "branches" are not literal branches nor the "fruit" literal fruit. There is no reason either why the "fire" must be literal fire. Instead it serves as an effective metaphor for whatever trials or hardships may attend the life of a lapsed disciple. "Fire" as a figure for temporal afflictions is a commonplace in the Bible and, indeed, in all of literature (see Deut. 32:22–24; Ps. 78:21; Isa. 9:18, 19; Jer. 15:14; Amos 1:4, 7, 10, 12; etc.).

Whether restoration of a branch to its former position in the vine is possible or not is a point that lies outside the scope of the metaphor. But it might be pointed out that the process of withering suggests a lapse of time prior to the experience of the fire itself. What is not possible in nature is, of course, possible with God. It is unwise to push a figure of speech too far or to require it to express ideas which it is not capable of bearing. It is sufficient to learn from our Lord's words that abiding is crucial to fruitfulness and that the failure to abide can lead to spiritual disaster.

Much perplexity has been generated by expositions of John 15 which either implicitly or explicitly identified its concepts with Paul's assertion that believers are "in Christ" (e.g., Eph. 1:3). But this identification is superficial and unwarranted. The conditional character of the abiding relationship should have told us that from the beginning.

It is extremely dangerous in the interpretation of Scripture to equate unthinkingly the meanings of words and expressions that are found in widely differing contexts. The equation of the "in Me" of John 15 with Paul's "in Christ" is only one case in point. Another which affects the present discussion involves John 10:27, 28. In those verses Jesus affirms:

"My sheep hear My voice, and I know them, and they follow Me. And I give them eternal life, and they shall never perish; neither shall anyone snatch them out of My hand."

It has been quite common to identify the term "follow" with the thought of discipleship, in which men are challenged to follow Christ. But again the identification cannot withstand scrutiny.

Few of those who hold that the word "follow" in John 10:27 must mean something like "obey" have stopped to ask a very relevant question. What accounts for the sequence here? Why does Jesus say, "They follow Me and I give to them eternal life," rather than, "I give to them eternal life and they follow Me"? It sounds as though the giving of eternal life is *the result of* His sheep following Him. As a matter of fact, this conclusion is undoubtedly correct!

A comparison of John 10:27, 28 with John 5:24 will show how natural this conclusion is within the familiar context of Johannine thought. John 5:24 contains several distinct elements: (1) the hearing of Christ's word; (2) faith; (3) the possession of eternal life; (4) a guarantee against judgment; (5) a secure situation ("passed from death into life"). All of these elements are echoed in John 10:27, 28. The only new feature is the expression, "I know them," which is contextually determined by the stress on Jesus' capacity to recognize His own sheep (10:14, 26). Leaving this aside, we have the following features in verses 27 and 28: (1) hearing Christ's voice; (2) following; (3) the giving of eternal life; (4) a guarantee against perishing; (5) a secure situation (in Jesus' hand).

This leads readily to the conclusion that in John 10:27 the term "follow" is simply another Johannine metaphor for saving faith. Like the metaphors about receiving (1:12), drinking (4:14), coming (6:35, 37), eating bread (6:35), eating Christ's flesh and drinking His blood (6:54) and others, it expresses the action in response to which eternal life is bestowed. When the Shepherd calls the sheep through His Word (and He knows who they are!), they respond to that call by following Him. That is to say, they commit their safety and well-being to the Shepherd who has summoned them to do so. A sheep's instinctive fear of strange voices lies of course in the background of this metaphor (see 10:4, 5), so that the decision to follow is after all an act of trust.

It is a mistake to construe the word "follow" in John 10:27 as though it indicates something about the nature of the believer's experience *after* he receives eternal life. In fact it has nothing to do with that at all, as its position in our Lord's utterance enables us to see. In the final analysis, John 10:27, 28 merely expresses in a fresh way the truth enshrined in John 5:24. The *immediately preceding* verses in John 10 suffice to show that the fundamental issue in Jesus' exchange with the Jews is *faith*. Thus in verses 25 and 26 Jesus tells them:

"I told you, and you do not **believe**. The works that I do in My Father's name, they bear witness of Me. But you do not **believe,** because you are not of My sheep, as I said to you" [emphasis added].

When John 10:27 is read in conjunction with these statements, its bearing is clear. These Jews are not His sheep because they do not *believe*, but His real sheep *follow*, i.e., they *believe!* Hence, John 10:27 and 28 have nothing to do with the subject of discipleship.

Expositors of God's Word are under a solemn responsibility to pay close attention to the exact nature of Scriptural declarations. The failure to do this is a primary reason why the theme of discipleship has often been confused with the Gospel of God's free saving grace. This confusion in turn has played into the hands of the Enemy with a resulting distortion of the terms on which man may obtain a place in heaven. It is high time for the Christian Church to renounce the theological errors that result from this and to reaffirm its commitment to the gift of God!

Only then can we be completely honest about the costs and dangers of true discipleship!

CHAPTER

5

1 John: Tests Of Life?

The Epistle of 1 John is the work of the same inspired writer who penned the Gospel of John. It is ironic that in the modern church it is often utilized in a way that is incompatible with the free offer of life found so repeatedly in the Fourth Gospel.

A major stream in the commentary tradition on 1 John holds that the epistle ought to be viewed as offering "tests of life." That is, John confronts his readership with questions about the quality of their Christian experience from which they may draw the conclusion that they either are, or are not, true believers. Should they fail to measure up, they have no reason to think that they possess eternal life.

It would be hard to devise an approach to John's first epistle more hopelessly misguided or more completely self-defeating. If the premise on which this approach is based were true, it would be quite impossible for either the original audience of 1 John or any of its subsequent readers to possess the assurance of salvation. Since the writer repeatedly enjoins the "abiding" life marked by

obedience to Christ's commands, one cannot really be certain until
the end of his earthly experience whether he has abided or per-
severed in the requisite obedience. Meanwhile, one must entertain
the possibility that he is a spurious Christian!

Few errors of contemporary exposition are more blatant than
this one. Not only does John *not* say that he is writing to "test"
whether his readers are saved or not, he says the reverse! This is
amply proved from a notable passage in the second chapter:

> I write to you, little children, **because your sins are
> forgiven you** for His name's sake. I write to you, fathers,
> **because you have known Him** who is from the begin-
> ning. I write to you, young men, **because you have
> overcome** the wicked one. I write to you, little children,
> **because you have known the Father**. I have written
> to you, fathers, **because you have known Him** who is
> from the beginning. I have written to you, young men,
> **because you are strong, and the word of God abides
> in you, and you have overcome** the wicked one (1
> John 2:12–14; emphasis added).

So far from writing to his readers because he, or they, need to
"test" the reality of their Christian experience, John writes precisely because that experience is real!

It should be carefully noted that the passage quoted above is
immediately followed by a solemn warning:

> Do not love the world or the things in the world. If anyone
> loves the world, the love of the Father is not in him. For
> all that is in the world—the lust of the flesh, the lust of
> the eyes, and the pride of life—is not of the Father but
> is of the world (2:15, 16).

Coming as this warning does directly after the reassuring words
of 2:12–14, the admonition tells us a great deal. It reveals, in fact,
that from John's point of view morality can be effectively enjoined

upon those who possess a certitude about their relationship to God. Morality is not the *grounds* for assurance, but the *fruit* of it.

Paul also thought the same thing. He can therefore exhort the Ephesian Christians "to walk worthy of the calling with which you were called" (Eph. 4:1). Or he can say, "Therefore, as the elect of God, holy and beloved, put on tender mercies, kindness, humbleness of mind, meekness, longsuffering" (Col. 3:12). He can also add, "forgiving one another . . . even as Christ forgave you, so you do also" (Col. 3:13).

It is a serious misconception, however widespread it may be, that godly living is undermined if believers know already that they belong to Christ forever. On the contrary, the joy and gratitude of an assured relationship to God are precisely the well-springs from which holiness most naturally arises. The New Testament writers, at least, believed this strongly, even if we do not!

The appeal which John makes to avoid the enticements of the world demonstrates his practical realism. He knows full well that the world possesses a deceptive attractiveness to which even true Christians may fall prey. In particular, in this epistle, he is concerned with the worldly point of view espoused by the false teachers against whom he writes. These antichrists, as he fittingly calls them (2:18, 22), "are of the world. Therefore they speak as of the world, and the world hears them" (4:5). The readers need to be reminded of their true relationship to Christ so that they may effectively resist the erroneous ideas to which they are being exposed.

One idea that the antichrists may have advanced was that the readers were not after all genuinely saved. If, as seems probable, the false teachers were the forerunners of the later gnostic heretics, this is very likely to have been one of their tenets. A strong streak of elitism ran through gnostic thought. The gnostics alone could look forward to eternal felicity (however they may have defined this). The antichrists probably suggested that the readers did not have eternal life at all, and that they needed to adopt the "gnosis" (knowledge) which the gnostics brought.

That something like this was indeed part of the problem is strongly hinted at toward the conclusion of John's first critique of the antichrists. This critique, which begins in 2:18, reaches its climax in 2:25–27. It is in verse 25 that John reminds his readers: "And this is the promise that He has promised us—eternal life." Having said this, he adds at once, "There things I have written to you concerning those who try to deceive you" (2:26). The conjunction of these two statements certainly makes it probable that the false teachers denied the divine promise about eternal life on which the readers were relying.

The readers, therefore, must be assured that, "I have not written to you because you do not know the truth, but because you know it, and that no lie is of the truth" (2:21). Their responsibility is to "let that abide in you which you have heard from the beginning" (2:24a). They are not to give way before the falsehoods they are now hearing. And if they do hold on to the Christian truth they already know, the abiding life will be their continuing experience. "If what you have heard from the beginning abides in you, you also will abide in the Son and in the Father" (2:24b).

But here, as we have already seen in John 8 and John 15, the abiding life is a contingent experience. In the words, "If what you have heard from the beginning abides in you," the writer formulates a Greek condition whose hypothetical form does *not* take the fulfillment of its terms for granted. John is perfectly sure that his readers are forgiven, know God, have experienced victory over the wicked one and know the truth, because he says so (2:12–14, 21). But he is *not* equally sure that the readership will not be seduced by the worldly spirit which they are now confronting.

This perspective is precisely the converse of the view that is so frequently taken of John's first epistle. So far from commanding his readers to "abide" in order to assure themselves that they are truly saved, he in fact assures them they are saved and challenges them on that basis to abide. How do they know they are saved? They have the divine promise of eternal life (2:25)!

If all of this is properly kept in mind, the reader of 1 John will be able to avoid a widespread misconception about a later statement found in 5:13. There the Apostle declares, "These things I have written to you who believe in the name of the Son of God, that you may know that you have eternal life. . . ." This assertion is very frequently, and wrongly, taken as a statement of purpose for the entire epistle. It assumes, without further enquiry, that the expression "these things" refers to the letter as a whole. But this is contrary to the writer's usage. In 2:1, the words "these things I write" clearly refer to the immediately preceding discussion of sin in 1:5–10. In 2:26, a comparable statement refers with equal clarity to the previous section about the antichrists. From these two earlier examples, we would naturally draw the conclusion that the "these things" of 5:13 is most likely to refer to the subject matter right before it.

This conclusion is fully justified by the content of 1 John 5:9–12. In fact, in these verses alone do we find in this epistle an explicit discussion that focuses directly on faith and eternal life. The passage deserves quotation:

> If we receive the witness of men, the witness of God is greater; for this is the witness of God which He has testified of His Son. He who believes in the Son of God has the witness in himself; he who does not believe God has made Him a liar, because he has not believed the testimony that God has given of His Son. And this is the testimony: that God has given us eternal life, and this life

> is in His Son. He who has the Son has life; he who does
> not have the Son of God does not have life (1 John
> 5:9–12).

It is to such assertions as these that John adds in verse 13, "These things I have written to you who believe in the name of the Son of God, *that you may know* that you have eternal life" (emphasis added).

Plainly in a passage like this we are breathing once again the atmosphere of the Fourth Gospel and of verses like John 5:24. There is nothing in 1 John 5:9–12 about "obedience" or "abiding" or anything else of that sort. Everything is made to hinge on whether or not we can accept God's testimony about His Son. Moreover, eternal life is seen as something God "has given" us in His Son—that is, as always for John, it is a divine gift. It is precisely these reaffirmations of the simple Gospel that are the grounds on which the Apostle expects his readers to *know* that they possess eternal life. To put it simply, they are to trust "the promise that He has promised" them (2:25)!

There is no reason, therefore, to seek the purpose of this epistle exclusively in 1 John 5:13 anymore than it is to be sought exclusively in 2:1 or 2:26. Instead, the most natural place to look for the overarching thrust of the letter is in its prologue. And there the purpose is defined clearly as "fellowship" with God. Thus it is that John writes:

> That which was from the beginning, which we have heard,
> which we have seen with our eyes, which we have looked
> upon, and our hands have handled, concerning the Word
> of life . . . that which we have seen and heard we declare
> to you, that you also may have fellowship with us; and
> truly our fellowship is with the Father and with His Son
> Jesus Christ (1:1, 3).

Much confusion could have been avoided in the study of John's epistle if this initial declaration of intent had been clearly kept in focus.

It almost goes without saying that "fellowship" is not to be defined as a virtual synonym for being a Christian. King David was surely a regenerate man when he committed adultery and murder, but he could not be said to have been in God's fellowship at the time! Even on a human plane, a son or daughter may lose fellowship with a parent even though they do not thereby lose the family relationship. The equation of "fellowship" with "being a Christian" (or something similar) is extremely far-fetched. Fellowship, like abiding, is a fully conditional relationship and this fact is sufficiently demonstrated by the statements found in 1:5–10.

Fellowship, of course, was precisely what was threatened by the advent of the antichrists. Since the readers had a divine promise about eternal life, nothing these false prophets could do or say could destroy the readers' fundamental relationship to God. But should the readership begin to listen to the doctrines of these men, their experience of fellowship with the Father and the Son would be in jeopardy. Up to now, the readers had apparently resisted the false teaching successfully (4:4). The Apostle wishes this resistance to continue (2:24–27).

Ironically, the antichrists with whom John is concerned had evidently emerged from the Apostolic circle itself. This is indicated by the statement in 2:19 which says:

> **They went out from us, but they were not of us; for if they had been of us, they would have continued with us; but they went out that they might be made manifest, that none of them were of us.**

That the "us" in this assertion is the Apostolic circle to which the writer belongs is shown by the immediate contrast with "you" found in verse 20. This "we"—"you" contrast appears for the first time in the prologue itself (1:1–3) and again, clearly, in 4:4–6. In the latter passage the "they" (4:5) refers to the antichrists, as it also does here in 2:19.

The false prophets had therefore seceded from the Apostolic communion, which probably means that they had once been a part of the Palestinian church. Jerusalem and Judea had long been the orbit of direct Apostolic influence and authority. But roots like this could give their teachings a seeming aura of respectability which might have a dangerous impact on the readership to whom they had come. In this respect, the errorists had something in common with the legalists of Acts 15:1, since these came to Antioch from Judea. The Jerusalem Council denied any connection with them (15:24) just as John does here.

The statement of 2:19 cannot rightly be taken as a generalized assertion related to the lifestyle of the born-again believer. John is talking in fact about heresy and defection from the faith and declaring that such defection would have been inconceivable if these individuals had truly shared the Apostles' spirit and perspective. His words bear a striking resemblance to the observation of the Apostle Paul in 1 Corinthians 11:18, 19:

> For first of all, when you come together in church, I hear that there are divisions among you, and in part I believe it. For there must also be heresies among you, that those who are approved may be recognized among you.

Paul's comment is instructive. Heresy and division, even among genuine Christians (he does *not* suggest that any of his readers are *not* Christians!), is designed by God to distinguish those who merit His approbation from those who do not. Heresy does not occur in a vacuum. Rather it unmasks deep spiritual deficiencies which otherwise might go undetected. This is essentially what John declares here as well. The secession of these false teachers unmasked their fundamental disharmony with the outlook of the Apostles. In that sense "they were not of us."

To say more than this is to go beyond the text. No doubt the antichrists *were* unsaved. But this is not the point. Even if they *had been* genuine believers, such a secession could not have taken place if—and as long as—they truly shared the Apostolic spirit and commitment to the truth. To make a general expression like "of us" mean something more specific than that is not warranted in any way.

The principal source of confusion in much contemporary study of 1 John is to be found in the failure to recognize the real danger against which the writer is warning. The eternal salvation of the readership is not imperilled. It is not even in doubt as far as the author is concerned. But seduction by the world and its antichristian representatives is a genuine threat which must be faced. Along with their heretical denials of the Person of Christ (2:22, 23; 4:1–3), the false teachers evidently also espoused a lifestyle that was basically worldly and unloving.

It is certainly not by chance that a general warning against the selfish and lustful spirit of the world (2:15–17) immediately precedes the first specific warning against the antichrists (2:18–27). Again, the second explicit caution against false prophets (4:1–6) is followed at once by an exhortation to "love one another" (4:7) and an extended passage on love (4:7–21). If the readers should begin to doubt the reality of their personal salvation and fundamental relationship to God, they will be the more easily enticed into the self-seeking lifestyle all around them. They must know, therefore, that they truly have eternal life (2:25; 5:13) and are called to experience fellowship with the Apostles themselves (1:3a) and with the Father and the Son (1:3b). To surrender such fellowship—they apparently had not done so as yet—would be to surrender the privilege of truly knowing God.

Naturally, from one point of view, fellowship with an individual is the essential medium for acquiring an intimate knowledge of that individual. Friends come to know friends, and even children come to know their parents, by means of shared time and experience—that is, through "fellowship." The same is true also at the level of our relationship to God. While it can be said that in one sense all true Christians know God (John 17:3), it is possible to conceive of a sense in which a true Christian may *not* know God.

This is made clear in a striking remark by the Lord Jesus Christ in John 14:7. There He declares to His disciples:

> "If you had known Me, you would have known My Father also; and from now on you know Him and have seen Him."

The format of the conditional sentence in Greek indicates (as the English does also), that up to this moment the disciples had—in a special sense—not really known Jesus or His Father. When Philip at once requests to see the Father (14:8), his ignorance about Christ is reaffirmed:

> Jesus said to him, "Have I been with you so long, and yet you have not known Me, Philip? He who has seen Me has seen the Father; so how can you say, "Show us the Father"? (14:9)

Despite the fact that Philip, along with the other disciples, had believed in Jesus (John 1:40–51; 2:11) and had eternal life, the Person of their Savior remained something of an enigma to them. They had not yet perceived how fully He reflected His Father (14:10) and, in this sense, they did not *know* Him!

Later in the same chapter Jesus offers a personal self-disclosure to His disciples which will be contingent on their obedience to His commands. His statement shows that He speaks of a future experience for them which will involve intimacy with Himself and His Father. His words are given in John 14:21–24:

> "He who has my commandments and keeps them, it is he who loves Me. And he who loves Me will be loved by

My Father, and I will love him and **manifest Myself** to him." Judas (not Iscariot) said to Him, "Lord, how is it that you **will manifest Yourself** to us, and not to the world?" Jesus answered and said to him, "If anyone loves Me, he will keep My Word; and My Father will love him, and We will come to him and **make Our home** with him. He who does not love Me, does not keep My words; and the word which you hear is not Mine but the Father's who sent Me" [emphasis added].

It should be plain from this passage that "fellowship" and "the knowledge of God" are implicit in the offer Jesus is making. Even the concept of the "abiding" life is evoked by the Greek word for "home" which is a cognate to the word for "abide." But everything depends on the love that the disciples have for their Lord, which is seen as the true source of obedience to His commands.

It is precisely this kind of truth that imbues so much of John's first epistle. "Fellowship" is its overriding theme and this means quite simply the "abiding" life marked by the self-disclosure of Christ—that is, by the knowledge of God. Hence, as in John 14:21-24, such an experience can only be claimed by those who obey Jesus' commandments (1 John 2:3-6). The readers need to keep this in mind not only with regard to any false claims to "knowledge" which they may have heard, but also with regard to their own personal lives as well.

Particularly striking in regard to the theme of "knowing God" is the assertion made in 1 John 4:7, 8:

Beloved, let us love one another, for love is of God; and everyone who loves is born of God and knows God. He who does not love does not know God, for God is love.

From this text it would be natural to deduce that "new birth" and "knowing God" are distinguishable experiences. If a man loves—in the Christian sense of that word—both experiences can be

predicated of him. If he does *not* love, all that John affirms is that
he does not *know* God. John does not say, however, that he is not
born of God!

It would have been easy for the Apostle to have said this, if he
had believed it. But when it comes to sin in Christian experience—
including the failure to love—John is a hardheaded realist. He is,
in fact, much more of a realist than many modern theologians.
There is no time, this author declares, when a Christian may say
he is sinless. Indeed, "If we say we have no sin, we deceive ourselves, and the truth is not in us" (1 John 1:8). One indication that
the truth has an effective hold on the Christian's heart is his
awareness that he is a sinful person. This, of course, must be
accompanied by a willingness to confess his sin whenever he de-
tects it (1:9). Not to do so is to hide from reality and to live in the
dark (cf. 1:5–7).

It has often been thought, however, that John contradicts his
earlier insistence on the reality of sin in a Christian's life by his
later words in 3:6 and 9. In those places, the Apostle writes:

**Whoever abides in him does not sin. Whoever sins has
neither seen Him nor known Him (3:6).**

**Whoever has been born of God does not do sin, for His
seed remains in him; and he cannot sin, because he has
been born of God (3:9, Greek).**

These statements are straightforward enough and ought not to be
watered down or explained away. Nevertheless, they do not contradict 1:8.

In modern times a popular expedient for dealing with the difficulties perceived in 1 John 3:6, 9 is to appeal to the use of the
Greek present tense. It is then asserted that this tense necessitates
a translation like, "Whoever has been born of God does not *go on*
sinning," or, "does not *continually* sin." The inference to be
drawn from such renderings is that, though the Christian may sin

somewhat (how much is never specified!), he may not sin regularly or persistently. But on all grounds, whether linguistic or exegetical, this approach is indefensible.

As has been pointed out by more than one competent Greek scholar, the appeal to the present tense invites intense suspicion. No other text can be cited where the Greek present tense, unaided by qualifying words, can carry this kind of significance. Indeed, when the Greek writer or speaker wished to indicate that an action was, or was not, continual, there were special words to express this.

But this is not all. The "tense solution" lands its proponents in insuperable difficulties and inconsistencies. Thus, if in 1:8 the present tense were read in this way, we would have the following: "If we say we do not *continually* have sin, we deceive ourselves and the truth is not in us." But if the tense explanation were correct, we ought to be able to say this without self-deception, since "whoever is born of God does not *continually* sin"! In the same way, if the tense is given this force in 5:16, we could read, "If anyone sees his brother *continually* sinning a sin . . . ." But how could someone see a brother *continually* sinning if one born of God does not *continually* sin?

It is apparent that the "tense solution" is a form of special pleading when it is applied to 1 John 3:6 and 9 because they are problems, but not applied elsewhere even to the same kind of idea. Nor would those who propose this kind of approach welcome its employment in other doctrinally significant places. As an example, John 14:6 might be handled as some wish to handle 1 John 3:6, 9. Then we could read this famous text as follows: "I am the way, the truth, and the life. No one *continually* comes to the Father except through Me." But the implication of this would be that *occasionally* someone might come another way! Obviously such an approach falsifies the text.

When the passage in which the statements in question occur is closely considered, it is clear that the writer intends them to be taken in an absolute sense. Immediately before verse 6, he affirms: "And you know that He was manifested to take away our sins, and in Him is no sin" (3:5). Clearly, the assertion "in Him is no sin" is an absolute denial of sin in the Son of God. But this is followed at once by the statement, "Whoever abides in Him does not sin." The point unmistakably is: if you abide in a sinless Person, you do not sin.

The same can really be said also of 1 John 3:9. The reason one who is born of God does not do sin is that "His seed remains in him; and he cannot sin, because he has been born of God." In other words, the regenerate one is sinless because He is begotten by a sinless Parent. It is completely contrary to the intent of the author to water such statements down. A sinless Parent does not beget a child who only sins a little! To say this, is in fact to deny what the text intends to convey.

But how are such claims to be harmonized with the direct assertion of 1:8 that no believer can claim to be sinless? There seems to be one simple way in which this can be done. The claims of 3:6 and 9 pertain to the believer when he is viewed only as "abiding" or as one who is "born of God." That is, sin is never the product of our abiding experience. It is never the act of the regenerate self per se. On the contrary, sin is the product of ignorance and blindness toward God. "Whoever sins has neither seen Him nor known Him" (3:6b). When a believer sins, he is acting out of darkness, not out of knowledge. He is acting as a man of flesh, not as a regenerate person.

Not surprisingly, even Paul could view sin as something intrinsically foreign to his true inner self. Thus, in recounting his personal struggle against sin in Romans 7, he can write:

> Now if I do what I will not to do, **it is no longer I who do it**, but sin that dwells in me. I find then a law, that evil

> is present with me, the one who wills to do good. For I
> delight in the law of God according to the inward man.
> But I see another law in my members, warring against
> the law of my mind, and bringing me into captivity to the
> law of sin which is in my members. O wretched man that
> I am! Who will deliver me from this body of death? I thank
> God—through Jesus Christ our Lord! So then, with the
> mind **I myself** serve the law of God, but **with the flesh**
> the law of sin (Rom. 7:20–25; emphasis added).

Here the Apostle achieves a self-perspective in which he can at
once admit that he sins and yet still say that "it is no longer I that
do it." His true self ("I myself," verse 25) serves God's law, even
while he confesses that "with the flesh" he serves the law of sin.

It is of great importance that this form of self-analysis precedes
the solution to his problem that is given in Romans 8. To view sin
as intrinsically foreign to what we are as regenerate people in
Christ is to take the first step toward spiritual victory over it.

From a slightly different perspective, the same conclusion is to
be deduced from a statement like that found in Galatians 2:20:
"I have been crucified with Christ; it is no longer I who live, but
Christ lives in me." But if only Christ truly lives, sin cannot be
a part of that experience at all! If the person in whom Christ lives
sins, that sin is in no way a part of that person's fundamental
life—since Christ is that life!

It is the final irony that the "tense solution" not only mishandles
the linguistics of the text, but undermines its true force and power.
By adopting an interpretation that tolerates a "moderate amount"
of sin, this view destroys the author's point. *All sin* is the fruit of
blindness and ignorance toward God (3:6b). It is Satanic since "the
devil has sinned from the beginning" (3:8). To make *any sin* less
than these things, is to soften its character and to prepare the
ground for tolerating it.

It follows, of course, that if the regenerate man *cannot* sin *at all* as a regenerate man (but only as an expression of his sinful flesh), he can never *manifest* his true inward nature by any other means than righteousness. By contrast, an unsaved man—a "child of the devil"—manifests his nature through sin. This is precisely what John goes on to say in 3:10a:

By this the children of God are manifest and the children of the devil [Greek].

The key word here is "manifest." A sinning Christian *conceals* his true character when he sins and *reveals* it only through holiness. On the other hand, a child of Satan *reveals* his true character by sin.

The words "by this" (3:10a, Greek) appear to round off the discussion found in 3:1-9. At 3:10b, a new thrust appears. It builds, of course, on what has just been said. If *all* sin—of whatever kind or extent!—is Satanic, it follows that it never finds its source in God. The one who does it, therefore, is not "of God" in the sinful thing that he does. This does not mean that such a person is unsaved. It means rather that he is acting outside of all vital contact with God. Satan, not God, is the source of his actions.

Therefore, John goes on to say:

Whoever does not do righteousness is not of God, nor is he who does not love his brother (3:10b, Greek).

That these words are intended for Christians is obvious on its face. The words "his brother" indicate this quite plainly. An unsaved man cannot hate *his* Christian brother since a true Christian is not really his brother. If John had had unregenerate people in mind, he could easily have said: "nor is he who does not love a brother." The fact that he personalizes the relationship with the word "his" cannot be overlooked.

Quite naturally John proceeds at once to appeal to the commandment given to Christians to "love one another" (3:11). He warns against brotherly hatred such as Cain exhibited toward Abel and stigmatizes such hatred as Satanic (3:12a). He touches a sensitive nerve when he suggests that this hatred can arise from the superior character of our brother's righteousness (3:12b). Such hatred is also worldly and its presence in people of the world should occasion no surprise (3:13). Only its presence in believers is abnormal!

At this point the writer slips into the first person plural: "*We* know that *we* have passed from death to life, because *we* love the brethren"(3:14a). This is followed by the warning that, "He who does not love his brother abides in death" (3:14b). It is likely enough that the "we" of the first half of the verse is the familiar Apostolic "we" of the epistle (cf. 1:1-5; 4:6). The writer would thus be claiming that love of the brethren marks the Apostolic circle to which he himself belongs. The Apostles find their experience in the sphere of "life." Anyone who hates *his* brother is living in the sphere of death to which also the world belongs.

It is quite true that the expression "passed from death to life" occurs elsewhere in John 5:24. But that is the only other place in the Johannine literature where it does occur outside of the present instance. It is, therefore, hardly a stereotyped expression. The context here suggests that John is using it in an experiential sense and not with reference to conversion as such. He and his fellow apostles know that they are in a sphere which can be described as "life" because they actually love their brothers in Christ. If anyone does not love *his* brother he is clearly "abiding" in the sphere of death. That is to say, he is out of touch with God. He is not living as a true disciple of his Master (cf. John 13:35).

There follows a verse that has perplexed many. In it John asserts:

Whoever hates his brother is a murderer, and you know that no murderer has eternal life abiding in him (3:15).

The view that a Christian cannot commit murder encounters insuperable obstacles. For one thing, King David was guilty of murder in a fully literal sense. Moreover, upon confession of that sin,

God forgave him (2 Samuel 12:13; see Psalm 51 and 1 John 1:9). Even Peter feels it necessary to warn his Christian readers against murder (1 Peter 4:15). In the face of such facts, it is plain that a genuine believer is not immune even to this sin.

If anyone were to maintain, nevertheless, that not only can a Christian not commit murder, but he cannot even hate his brother, such a view would be totally lacking in Biblical realism. It is also quite contrary to actual Christian experience, as any man who is fully honest must confess.

But John does not say that a murderer does not *have* eternal life. He says that a murderer does not have eternal life *abiding* in him. Since for John eternal life is nothing else than Christ Himself (cf. John 14:6; 1 John 1:2 and 5:20), this is the same as saying that "no murderer has *Christ* abiding in him."

Thus the key word in 1 John 3:14, 15 is once again the word "abide." In the sense in which this is used in John 15 and everywhere in this epistle, this is a contingent experience dependent upon the Christian's obedience to God's commands. If a believer disobeys the command to "love one another" (3:11), he cannot claim to be "abiding" in the sphere of "life" or to have God's life "abiding" in him. Hatred breaks our experiential contact with the life of Christ, plunges us into spiritual darkness and endows us with a quality of existence which can best be described as "death."

As always, Paul also thought this way as well. When he attempted to live the Christian life under the law he discovered that "sin, taking occasion by the commandment, deceived me and by it killed me" (Rom. 7:11). Indeed, speaking of Christians explicitly he affirms:

> And if Christ is in you, the body is dead because of sin, but the Spirit is life because of righteousness (Rom. 8:10).

But if even the Christian's body may be called dead in a spiritual sense, what will the Christian experience if he lives according to the dictates of that body? The answer is obvious: he will have an experience that can be described as death. Thus Paul goes on to warn: "For if you live according to the flesh you will die" (Rom. 8:13).

It may be affirmed, therefore, that the Christian only *experiences* the eternal life God has freely given him when he is obedient to God. All else is an experience of death—at a spiritual level, first of all, but if continued in long enough, at a physical level as well (Jam. 1:15; Prov. 11:19; etc.). In 1 John 3:10b-15, the Apostle's point is really quite simple. The failure to love one's brother is not a true experience of eternal life at all. It is an experience of moral murder and of death. This is putting it quite starkly, but it furnishes an effective antidote to inward tendencies which every honest believer will admit that he has.

To return, therefore, to the statement of 1 John 4:7, if a man truly loves his fellow Christians he shows thereby that he is both "born of God and knows God." If he does not, then he surely does not really know God at the level of real fellowship and intimacy with Christ. Of course, the unsaved world does not know God either, and the believer who harbors hatred toward another believer is stepping into a comparable sphere of spiritual darkness and death. This by no means calls his salvation into question, but it firmly negates every claim to intimacy with the Father and the Son. In the final analysis, it is this intimacy that the epistle of 1 John is all about (1:3, 4)!

In conclusion, therefore, it must be pointed out that the first epistle of John is both internally consistent and fully harmonious with the uncomplicated offer of eternal life which is so frequently propounded in the Fourth Gospel. But the epistle will continue to be misunderstood by those who insist on equating "fellowship" and "abiding" with "regeneration" and "being a Christian." Once these unjustified equations are made, the message of John's letter is hopelessly obscured. The theological deductions that arise as a result are fundamentally and irreconcilably hostile to the simple Biblical Gospel and to the offer of assurance of salvation based on the testimony and promise of God alone.

It is in this way that the Apostle's lovely letter about fellowship has been sadly misconstrued and put into the service of the siege of the Gospel!

CHAPTER

6

The Christian and Apostasy

Few questions in the Bible are more shocking than the one recorded in Matthew 11:3: "Are You the Coming One, or do we look for another?"

The reason we find this query astounding is because it came from none other than John the Baptist himself. The man who asked it, therefore, was the same one who had once exclaimed, "Behold! The Lamb of God who takes away the sin of the world!" (John 1:29). It was he who had also declared, "And I have seen and testified that this is the Son of God" (John 1:34). It is clear that the faith evident in these earlier affirmations by this great prophet was not present in the question, "Are You the Coming One?"

Of course, John was in prison at the time (Matt. 11:2). No doubt his drained physical and mental condition contributed to the doubts he now entertained. But one thing is plain. For the moment, his faith in Christ had failed.

Was he therefore now a lost man? Of course not. To the woman at the well of Sychar, to the rabbi Nicodemus, to all His hearers, Jesus had offered a gift appropriated by faith. It was the gift that was indefectible, not the faith that laid hold of it to begin with. "But the water that I shall give him [not the faith that claims it!] will become in him a well of water springing up into everlasting life" (John 4:14).

It is widely held in modern Christendom that the faith of a genuine Christian cannot fail. But this is not an assertion that can be verified from the New Testament. On the contrary, we learn the opposite from a statement like that found in 2 Timothy 2:17, 18:

> And their message will spread like cancer. Hymenaeus and Philetus are of this sort, who have strayed concerning the truth, saying that the resurrection is already past, and they **overthrow the faith** of some [emphasis added].

The Apostle Paul, therefore, knew of actual cases where the faith of individuals had actually been overthrown by false teaching. Yet, as the following verse makes clear, Paul is sure that such a calamity does not affect anyone's eternal destiny since "the solid foundation of God stands, having this seal: 'The Lord knows those who are His' " (2:19a).

It is obviously true, of course, that God knows *who* are His. But this observation is so self-evident that it is not likely to be Paul's meaning. Instead, the Greek word for "know" can imply relationship and the Apostle's affirmation is best understood in this sense. God knows intimately and personally all who stand in relationship to Himself. This fact is undisturbed even when the believer's faith wavers or is overthrown.

Moreover, the reality just stated in no way compromises God's holiness. His demand remains unaffected: "Let everyone who names the name of Christ depart from iniquity" (2:19b). But it should be noted that this assertion is a *command*, while the one preceding it is a statement of fact. It is not said that the command is always heeded. The following verses (2:20–21) show that in God's house it is *not* always heeded. Nevertheless the demand remains.

Here then is a fundamental passage on the defectibility of human faith and the indefectibility of God's relationship to those who exercise that faith. To confuse the stability of a man's faith with the stability of God's purposes is to confuse two different things. Naturally, such confusion leads inevitably to doctrinal error.

If this simple distinction had been kept in mind, the Epistle to the Hebrews could have been taken by the Church at face value and its solemn warnings against apostasy could have had their intended effect. Instead, that epistle has suffered much at the hands of expositors who felt—no doubt sincerely—that true Christians could not really succumb to the dangers the writer of Hebrews describes.

As is well known, in Hebrews 6:4, 5, the author describes individuals "who were once enlightened, and have tasted the heavenly gift, and have become partakers of the Holy Spirit, and have tasted the good word of God and the powers of the age to come." That such expressions naturally describe real Christians will be obvious to all who have not already decided that the remainder of the passage cannot. It seems almost needless to refute in detail the efforts made to show that unregenerate people are in view here. All such efforts are strained and unconvincing.

Perhaps, however, it is worth observing that the attempt to see in the word "tasted" an inadequate appropriation is clearly without foundation in this epistle. According to the author, "Jesus . . . was made a little lower than the angels . . . that He, by the grace of God, might taste death for everyone" (Heb. 2:9). No one will maintain that the Savior's "taste" of death was anything but the most profound experience thereof. The idea of "tasting" is, in fact, a recognizable Biblical figure for genuine appropriation of God's goodness (see 1 Peter 2:1–3; Psalm 34:8). To take the word in another sense in Hebrews 6:4, 5 has no sound exegetical basis whatsoever.

Additionally, the Greek verb for "enlightened" (6:4) is used again later in the letter to describe the readers' conversion experience ("illuminated," 10:32), while the term "partakers" (6:4) also describes their relationship to their heavenly calling (3:1). On all grounds the effort to see unsaved people in this text is extremely unnatural.

But of those whom he describes in 6:4, 5, the writer also affirms that they can "fall away." The directness of this affirmation is masked by the familiar English rendering, "if they shall fall away" (6:6). Actually there is no word for "if" in the Greek text and none is required in the English translation. The verbal form which is rendered "fall way" is a Greek participle which stands last in a series of participles. The first of these participles is represented by the words "those who were once enlightened" (verse 4). We ought therefore to translate as follows:

> **For it is impossible to renew to repentance those who were once enlightened, and have tasted the heavenly gift, and have become partakers of the Holy Spirit, and have tasted the good word of God and the powers of the age to come, and have fallen away** . . . .

The writer clearly talks as if he knew of such cases.

We should not, however, construe "falling away" here as though it meant the loss of eternal life. This equation—frequently made—is unwarranted. The author repeatedly urges his readers to maintain their Christian profession and confidence (cf. 3:6, 12-

15; 6:11, 12; 10:23–25). The man who falls away is evidently the one who casts that confidence, and its attendant reward, aside (10:35). Here again we meet the defectibility of human faith. Man's faith needs continual nurture and admonition.

Of the man who falls away, the author affirms that it is impossible to "renew him to repentance." This suggests a hardness of heart which is impervious to all attempts to woo the man back to faith. But the writer probably thinks only of the normal efforts which other Christians may make to do this. The impossibility can hardly be said to apply to God. In fact, in his metaphor which follows, the author deftly implies the possibility of restoration after punishment has been experienced.

The image which he employs describes a field which partakes of the rain of heaven and brings forth fitting fruits (6:7). In that case, the field enjoys divine blessing. On the other hand, "if it bears thorns and briars, it is rejected and near to being cursed, whose end is to be burned" (6:8). The burning of fields was a practice known in antiquity and would doubtless be a familiar idea to the readers of the epistle. But this practice was not designed to destroy the field, but to destroy the unacceptable growth which made it unfruitful. By utilizing such an illustration the author clearly signals the ultimate purpose of the divine judgment on the apostate Christian. That purpose is restoration to fruitfulness.

This in no way makes the anticipation of judgment a pleasant one. On the contrary, it is a fearful expectation (cf. 10:26, 27). The guilt of the apostate is enormous since his renunciation of faith is like a personal re-crucifixion of God's Son in which his Savior is openly shamed once again (6:6b). His life as an apostate meets with divine rejection and falls under a curse which is realized in the retribution to which he is now exposed (6:8). One might recall in this connection the "curses" which fell on God's

Old Testament people as a result of their disobedience to the covenant of their God (see Deuteronomy 27:9–26).

Hebrews 10:26–39 must be understood in essentially the same way. This famous passage follows a call to "hold fast the confession of our hope without wavering" (10:23) and a warning against "forsaking the assembling of ourselves together, as is the manner of some" (10:25). The "willful" sinning of 10:26 is thus to be understood specifically of this kind of sin—namely, abandonment of the Christian faith and of the church. And this is explicitly said to be "after we have received the knowledge of the truth." In other words, the writer again addresses the problem of apostasy.

It is possible that the readers of Hebrews were being allured by some form of Judaism in which there were still animal sacrifices. But the author warns that to abandon Christianity is to abandon the only sacrifice (the death of Christ) which affords real protection and that apart from this "there no longer remains a sacrifice for sins" (10:26b). To take so fateful a step is to stand exposed to God's "fiery indignation." It is to range oneself with "the adversaries" of the Christian faith and to share in their calamities (10:27). But nothing in verses 26 and 27 ought to be construed as a reference to hell.

The punishment which the author envisages for the apostate will be a "worse punishment" than the summary execution which offenders against the Mosaic law experienced (10:28, 29a). Of course, there are many forms of retribution which are fundamentally "worse" than swift death. The writer of Lamentations gives eloquent expression to this reality (Lam. 4:6, 9). One thinks easily of the mental disorder that afflicted Saul in the period of his declining years. Lingering illness, loss of loved ones and many other experiences might be thought of. The writer, however, is not concerned with being specific. He is only concerned with warning about the severity of the retribution which an apostate has in store for him.

But it is precisely because the apostate is a Christian that his crime is so great. This point is forcefully driven home by the words of verse 29:

> Of how much worse punishment, do you suppose, will he be thought worthy who has trampled the Son of God underfoot, counted the blood of the covenant **by which he was sanctified** a common thing, and insulted the Spirit of grace [emphasis added].

In the words "by which he was sanctified" the writer makes it inescapable that he is speaking of Christians.

The author has already spoken about sanctification in the immediately preceding context of Hebrews 10. His statements show clearly what he means by this idea. They are these:

> By that will we have been sanctified through the offering of the body of Jesus Christ once for all (10:10).
>
> For by one offering He has perfected forever those who are sanctified (10:14).

It follows, then, that in describing the apostate as one who has "counted the blood of the covenant by which he was sanctified a common thing," the writer is describing one who has been "perfected forever"! Precisely for this reason, his apostasy is an enormous offense against divine grace and merits the "worse punishment" which is threatened for this.

The effort to deny that a real Christian is in view here can only be described as a refusal to face the author's real meaning. The explanation that the "he" in the expression "by which he was sanctified" refers to Christ has absolutely nothing to commend it. No impartial reader could so construe the text. Furthermore, in Hebrews, Christ is not described as sanctified, but as the Sanctifier

(2:11). The writer of Hebrews obviously believes that a true Christian can apostatize.

The remainder of the passage (10:30–36) reinforces this point. Vengeance and judgment await the apostate (verses 30–31). But the readers can be strengthened against such failure by the recollection of their former fidelity in time of trial (verses 32–34). This past confidence is to be maintained now: "Therefore do not cast away your confidence, which has great reward" (verse 35). What they need is "endurance" so that they may accomplish God's will and receive the reward He has promised (verse 36). The coming of Christ draws near (verse 37) and this should give them courage to hold on.

Of particular interest is the statement of verse 38:

Now the just shall live by faith; but if he draws back, my soul has no pleasure in him.

The words are drawn from Habakkuk 2:3, 4 and incorporate the famous Pauline proof text about justification by faith. But the writer does not introduce this quotation with a formula of citation and for a good reason. What he has done is to alter the form of the Old Testament reference in a way that fits the context of his thought. In that sense the assertion of verse 38 is more strictly an Old Testament "allusion" than an Old Testament "quotation." But in this altered form it is plain that it is the "just" one who may draw back! If so, of course, God will not be pleased with him. This observation is a figure of speech called litotes in which a positive idea is expressed by negating its opposite. As the larger context makes plain, he means, "God will be severely angered" (see verse 27).

Verse 39 is misleading in its present English form. The Greek word for "perdition" is not—as is sometimes claimed—a technical term for "hell." Instead it may be used of simple waste (Matt. 26:8; Mk. 14:4) or of execution (Acts 25:16). In secular Greek its fundamental meanings were "destruction," "ruin," and similar ideas. Likewise, the particular Greek expression rendered "the saving of the soul" does not occur elsewhere in Biblical Greek. It is not the same Greek phrase which we met in James 1:21. But the precise phrase used here is found in classical Greek with the meaning "to save the life." The verse might be more appropriately rendered:

> But we for our part [the Greek pronoun is emphatic] are not of those who draw back to ruin, but of those who have faith for the saving of our life.

In this sense the verse coheres perfectly with the larger context. The apostate faces disaster and ruin. His punishment may not be swift execution as under Moses' law (cf. 10:28), but the judgment he experiences could easily end in death as other sin also does (James 1:15; 5:20; Rom. 8:13). But faith is the means by which the "just one" lives and is therefore indispensable to the preservation of his life (cf. 10:38).

From verse 32 through 36 the author has used the second person plural "you" to address his readers. The swift shift to an emphatic "we" in verse 39 appears to be a reference to himself. The cultured, literary "we" is the author's regular way of indicating himself (see 2:5; 5:11; 6:9, 11; 8:1; 13:18). The writer will then be affirming his own intention to hold on to his Christian profession and hope. He thus means something like: "But we ourselves (= I myself) do not belong among the number who draw back, but among those who preserve their lives by a continuing faith."

It is a fitting conclusion to a passage on the "willfull" sin of apostasy. The step against which he cautions can only be taken deliberately, and the refusal to take it is equally deliberate. The author has definitely decided not to take it! He trusts that his readers will refuse to do so as well.

The Epistle to the Hebrews, therefore, is fundamentally concerned with the problem of those who draw back from their

Christian commitment and conviction. Those who do so, of course, abandon the church (cf. 10:25). It is therefore the *visible household of faith* from which they secede. They cannot secede from the family of God, however, and precisely for this reason they are subject to God's discipline.

If the epistle is read in this way, it offers no fundamental problems at all. It clashes in no way with the basic truths of the Gospel. Christians in the church are in active partnership with the Apostle and High Priest of their Christian profession. The word "partakers" used in 3:1 to describe this relationship is exactly the word for business partners and this is its actual meaning in its only New Testament occurrence outside of Hebrews (Luke 5:7). It is common in the papyri in this sense. But "partnership" with Christ is a priestly occupation in which there is a spiritual altar that offers spiritual food (13:10) and in which there are spiritual sacrifices to be made (13:15, 16). One must hold on to this role.

If the Christian secedes from the visible, functioning priestly household—that is, from the church itself—he ceases to be a "partner of Christ." This is the meaning of the statement in 3:14 where the word for "partaker" is the same word as that used in verse 1. We thus constitute ourselves a part of this visible, functioning "house" only so long as we in fact "hold fast the confidence and the rejoicing of hope firm to the end" (3:6). To withdraw is to cast away the privileges that belong to the "house" much as a son who leaves home ceases to be an active partner in that home, though he does not thereby cease to be a son!

No doubt the warnings of Hebrews against abandonment of the faith are sharp and forceful. But this is no reason to deny that they apply to us. Indeed, this kind of denial would rob them of the impact they were intended to have. When the admonitory sections of the epistle are redirected toward supposed "false professors of faith," they are in reality distorted. The author of Hebrews shows not the slightest trace of a belief that his audience might contain unsaved people. Instead, he persistently addresses them as brethren (3:1, 12; 10:19; 13:22) who share the heavenly calling (3:1) and who have an High Priest through whom they can approach the throne of grace (4:14–16). The inference that he nevertheless thinks some of his audience to be unregenerate is not founded on true exegesis of the text.

No doubt the conclusions reached in this chapter will be stoutly resisted by those who cannot believe that a Christian could abandon his faith. But it must be pointed out that the refusal to admit this possibility remains an obvious begging of the question. The view that a Christian cannot apostatize is at bottom a theological, rather than an exegetical, conviction. Since it is not supported by the Bible, it ought to be given up.

When this is done, many passages can be read in their normal sense and the warnings they contain can be directly faced. Moreover, we can then also hear a note of hope for those whose faith has suffered shipwreck. It is such a note that sounds in the solemn statements Paul makes in 1 Timothy 1:19, 20:

> . . . holding faith and a good conscience, which some having rejected, concerning the faith have suffered shipwreck, of whom are Hymenaeus and Alexander, whom I have delivered to Satan that they may learn not to blaspheme.

What is striking here is that the Greek word translated "learn" literally means "to be trained," "to be educated." It is the normal Greek word for the education of a child who is a minor. Its only other uses by Paul are all in reference to Christians (1 Cor. 11:32; 2 Cor. 6:9; 2 Tim 2:25; Titus 2:12). 2 Timothy 2:25 is no exception to this.

Clearly the most natural inference here is that Paul regarded Hymenaeus and Alexander as Christians whose false doctrine amounted to blasphemy. They are now under divine discipline for which Satan is the instrument. One might compare with this Paul's similar concept in 1 Corinthians 5:4, 5. Paul hopes that the outcome of this spiritual education will be that these men will renounce their false doctrine. It is quite natural to suspect that this Hymenaeus is the same as the one mentioned in 2 Timothy 2:17 and who taught that the resurrection was already past. Whether in the end the discipline had a positive effect on either himself, or Alexander, is a matter on which the Scripture is silent. But the element of hope remains, just as it did also in the metaphor of the field in Hebrews 6:7, 8.

Nevertheless, the tragic dangers of doctrinal shipwreck remain a grim reality in the history of the Church and in its contemporary experience. A disservice is done to the cause of Christ when it is claimed that such dangers do not exist for real Christians.

"Therefore let him who thinks he stands take heed lest he fall" (1 Cor. 10:12)!

CHAPTER

7

Problem Passages in Paul

Certain passages in the Pauline letters have been taken to prove that good works are an inevitable outcome of genuine saving faith. As has already been pointed out, this kind of deduction destroys the believer's ground of assurance. A man who must wait for works to verify his faith cannot know until life's end whether or not his faith was real. This leads to the absurd conclusion that a man can believe in Christ without knowing whether he has believed in Christ!

Naturally the Pauline texts in question are all consistent with his fundamental doctrine of justification by faith and apart from works. When the Apostle writes that it is "not by works of righteousness which we have done, but according to His mercy He saved us" (Tit. 3:5), his true conviction comes through clearly. Paul could never have so expressed himself if he had regarded works as the real means by which we can know we are saved. To the contrary, he directs our focus away from the works *we* have done to the mercy of *God*. How can anyone read Paul and still believe that we can only be sure of God's mercy by our works?

Similarly, Paul also writes, "But to him who *does not work* but believes on Him who justifies the ungodly, his faith is counted for righteousness" (Rom. 4:5; emphasis added). Can anyone imagine that Paul would then go on to add, "But you need to work or you will not know whether you have been justified or not"! Such a proposition is a monstrous distortion of Pauline truth. Any articulation of the gospel which can affirm such a thing ought to be forcefully rejected by the Christian Church.

In the next few pages some Pauline statements will be examined which are alleged to lead to such a result. A few others will be considered in Chapter 9 in connection with the subject of heirship. The first text that can claim attention here is Galatians 6:8.

Galatians 6:8

In Galatians 6:7-9 Paul writes as follows:

> Do not be deceived, God is not mocked; for whatever a man sows, that he will also reap. For he who sows to his flesh will of the flesh reap corruption, but he who sows to the Spirit will of the Spirit reap everlasting life. And let us not grow weary while doing good, for in due season we shall reap if we do not lose heart.

It is important to see exactly what this text says. "Everlasting life," Paul asserts, is the direct consequence of sowing to the Spirit, of doing good. Corruption is what you reap if you do evil. It is all part of the law of the harvest. A man gets what he deserves to get!

It goes almost without saying that there is nothing said here about the "inevitable" results of saving faith. Indeed, the hortatory thrust of the passage shows the opposite. The Galatians must be careful about how they sow. They must never suppose that they can "mock" God or avoid the inexorable law of the harvest. The final reaping is not a foregone conclusion, but rather it is contingent on not "growing weary" while doing good.

But equally there is nothing here about justification by faith or the concept of a free gift. Nothing is plainer than that the "everlasting life" of which Paul speaks is not free, but based on the moral merits of those who reap it. To deny this is to deny the most obvious aspect of the text.

All becomes clear, however, if we simply remember that the Apostle is addressing believers (see, for example, 3:2–5) who have already been justified by faith and who possess everlasting life as a free gift. Naturally Paul knew that eternal life was freely given (Rom. 6:23; see also Rom. 5:15–18) just as the Apostle John knew this. But Paul is not speaking about what the Galatians *already have*, but about what they may *yet receive*. Herein lies the key to this text.

It must not be forgotten that eternal life is nothing less than the very life of God Himself. As such it cannot be thought of as a mere static entity. Rather its potentialities are rich beyond the power of the mind to conceive them. Thus we find Jesus declaring, "I have come that they may have life, and that they may have it more abundantly" (John 10:10). From this we learn that eternal life can be experienced in more than one measure or degree.

But it cannot be experienced at all unless first received as a free gift. Not surprisingly, the Creator of the Universe has illustrated this with every human life that is born into the world. No man or woman possesses physical life at all except by the benefaction of his parents. Even physical life is, therefore, a free gift! But when a child is born into the sphere of earth, the capacities of that life—all present at birth—must be developed by himself under the tutelage of his parents. How "abundantly" he will experience that life is determined by his response to instruction and to experience itself.

So also in the spiritual realm. To have life "more abundantly" is to experience it under those conditions where it can naturally flourish. For this, it cannot be surprising that obedience to our divine Parent is essential.

Here it should be clearly stated that in the New Testament eternal life is presented both as a free gift and as a reward merited by those who acquire it. But one important distinction always holds true. Wherever eternal life is viewed as a reward, its acquisition is assigned to a time in the future. But wherever eternal life is presented as a gift, its acquisition is assigned to the present. Naturally, it goes without saying that no one can ever receive it as a reward who does not first accept it as a free gift. This is the same as saying that a person must first *have* life before he can experience it richly.

If Galatians 6:8 is construed as speaking only of a man's final salvation from hell, then it teaches clearly that this final salvation is by works! Not to admit this is not to be candid. But no one excludes works from his doctrine of salvation more vigorously than Paul does, and he insists that to mix works and grace is to alter the character of both (see Romans 6:6). Galatians 6:8 is irreconcilable with fundamental Pauline truth so long as one holds the view that final salvation is under discussion.

But why hold this view? It is easy to understand how the measure and extent of one's experience of God's life must depend on the measure of his response to God. From that perspective the image of a harvest is exactly right. Both the nature and quantity of the seed we sow determines the nature and quantity of the harvest. It is obviously wise for a Christian to be reminded that every act he performs is like a seed sown in a field. Its harvest will be either corruption or eternal life. And is there a Christian alive who has not sown much more often to his flesh than he ought to have done? Clearly the Church needs this reminder about the law of life. To make the issue here a man's final destiny in heaven or hell is to lose the whole point of the admonition.

If the considerations just discussed in connection with Galatians 6:8 are kept in mind, other passages which offer eternal life as a future experience based on works can be understood in their proper bearing. One might think especially of Romans 2:6, 7 and Matthew 19:29 with its parallels in Mark 10:30 and Luke 18:30. The eschatological "harvest" is in view in all these places. Obedient men reap an experience of eternal life precisely because they are obedient. But this in no way conflicts with the reality that such obedience is preceded by—and motivated through—a gift of life given freely and without conditions.

Colossians 1:21-23

Perseverance in the faith has sometimes been deduced from Colossians 1:23 as a condition for final salvation. The passage in question reads as follows:

> And you, who once were alienated and enemies in your mind by wicked works, yet now He has reconciled in the body of His flesh through death, to present you holy, and blameless, and irreproachable in His sight—if indeed you continue grounded and steadfast in the faith, and are not moved away from the hope of the gospel which you have heard. . . .

It is clear that "condition" is the only appropriate word here. There is nothing to support the view that perseverance in the faith is an inevitable outcome of true salvation. On the contrary, the text reads like a warning. Naturally, in the context of the Colossian heresy (Col. 2:8, 16–23) that is exactly what it is!

But once again the mistake is made of referring the statement of the text to a man's final salvation. Words like "holy," "blameless," and "irreproachable" do not require an absolutist construction. Men can be described in all these ways who are not

completely sinless and the word "irreproachable" is actually in
the Pauline list of qualifications for deacons and elders (1 Tim.
3:10; Tit. 1:6, 7). A comparison of Colossians 1:22 with 1:28 is
particularly instructive.

In 1:28 Paul writes thus:

> Him we preach, warning every man and teaching every
> man in all wisdom, that we may present every man per-
> fect in Christ Jesus.

This statement is connected with 1:22 by the presence of the
special word "present." But here Paul employs the word "perfect"
which is the normal Greek word for "mature" (and is so used in
1 Cor. 2:6; 14:20; Heb. 5:14). Obviously this word also does not
have to suggest sinless perfection.

It is natural, therefore, to see 1:22 and 1:28 as slightly different
forms of the same idea. The aim of Christ's reconciling work at
the cross is the aim Paul serves by his teaching ministry. He seeks
to bring men to that matured experience of holiness which will
enable them to be presented acceptably to God. When they stand
on review before Him their lives ought to meet with His approbation (see also Rom. 14:10–12; 2 Cor. 5:10). But this can only be
achieved, he cautions his readers, if they hold firmly to their faith
in the Gospel and do not allow new ideas and doctrines to move
them away from fundamental truths.

As we have seen already, Paul knew perfectly well that Christians were not immune to the influences of heresy (2 Tim. 2:17–19;
1 Tim. 1:18–20). He is saying, then, that the Colossians will never
reach maturity in holiness if they listen to the wrong voices. In
that event, they could not be presented to God in a spiritual state
which truly fulfilled the aims of the cross. Their lives would be
open to His censure. They are, therefore, to hold firmly to the
faith they had heard from the beginning.

But of perseverance in the faith as a condition for final salvation from hell, Paul here says nothing at all.

1 Corinthians 15:2

It might be thought, however, that such an idea *does* find expression in 1 Corinthians 15:1, 2. There Paul writes:

> Moreover, brethren, I declare to you the gospel which I preached to you, which also you have received and in which you stand, by which also you are saved, if you hold fast that word which I preached to you—unless you believed in vain.

The problem with understanding this verse correctly rests chiefly in the English translation. A very flexible Greek verb *(katechō)* is rendered "hold fast" (in the AV it is translated "keep in memory"). But the verb could equally well be rendered "take hold of" and in that case it would refer to the act of appropriating the truth of the Gospel by faith.

Closer scrutiny of the Greek text suggests that this is indeed the correct understanding. The Greek word order can be represented as follows: "by which also you are saved, by that word I preached to you, if you take hold of it, unless you believed in vain." From this it appears that Paul is thinking of the saving effect of the preached word when it is duly appropriated, unless in fact that appropriation (by faith) has been in vain.

What he means by believing "in vain" is made clear in verses 14 and 17:

> And if Christ is not risen, then our preaching is vain and your faith is also vain.
> And if Christ is not risen, your faith is futile; you are still in your sins.

Thus 1 Corinthians 15:2 must be read in the light of the subsequent discussion about resurrection. Paul is simply saying, in verse 2, that the Gospel he has preached to them is a saving Gospel when

it is appropriated in faith, unless after all the resurrection is false—
in which case no salvation has occurred at all and the faith his
readers had exercised is futile. But naturally Paul absolutely insists
on the reality of the resurrection of Christ. He therefore does not
think that the Corinthians have believed "in vain."

But neither here nor anywhere else in the Pauline letters can
the Apostle be correctly construed as teaching that perseverance
in the faith is a condition for, or an indispensable sign of, final
salvation from hell.

1 Corinthians 1:8

In the opening chapter of his first letter to the Corinthian
church, Paul speaks positively and hopefully about the church's
spiritual prospects. The context shows clearly that he is speaking
of the church corporately:

> I thank my God always concerning you for the grace of
> God which was given to you by Christ Jesus, that you
> were enriched in everything by Him in all utterance and
> all knowledge, even as the testimony of Christ was con-
> firmed in you, so that you come short in no gift, eagerly
> waiting for the revelation of our Lord Jesus Christ, who
> will also confirm you to the end, that you may be blame-
> less in the day of our Lord Jesus Christ. God is faithful,
> by whom you were called into the fellowship of His Son,
> Jesus Christ our Lord (1 Cor. 1:4–9).

The Corinthian church is here praised because it is so richly
endowed with spiritual gifts, because the testimony of Christ has
received confirmation in the church's life and experience, and
because it waits eagerly for the coming of Christ. Paul fully expects God to bring the church to the place where it is blameless
before Him (the letter shows the church has a long way to go!)
and he bases this expectation on God's faithfulness. Paul is sure

that the myriad problems at Corinth, which he is about to discuss, can be worked out.

It would be a mistake to read more into the text than that. There is not to be found here a guarantee that each and every Christian individual will necessarily be brought to the place where his Christian life is "blameless" before God. (The word "blameless" is the same one we have met as "irreproachable" in Colossians 1:22.) In Paul's mind no such guarantee existed.

This is made perfectly plain in this very letter. Thus in chapter 3 the Apostle describes the assessment of the Christian's life and work which will someday take place at the Judgment Seat of Christ (see again, Rom. 14:10-12; 2 Cor. 5:10). His words are these:

> For no other foundation can anyone lay than that which is laid, which is Jesus Christ. Now if anyone builds on this foundation with gold, silver, precious stones, wood, hay, straw, each one's work will become manifest; for the Day will declare it, because it will be revealed by fire; and the fire will test each one's work, of what sort it is. If anyone's work which he has built on it endures, he will receive a reward. If anyone's work is burned, he will suffer loss; but he himself will be saved, yet so as through fire (1 Cor. 3:11 to 15).

It is transparent from this text that Paul entertained the possibility that in the Day of divine assessment, a Christian's work might be "burned up." The Greek verb employed in verse 15 (the one rendered "burned") is in fact an intensive word like our own verb "burned down." Should a Christian's works suffer such a fate, Paul affirms that his eternal destiny nevertheless will not be affected. "But he himself will be saved, yet so as through fire."

This assertion is so straightforward that it is absolutely amazing how widely it has been ignored. Obviously, if a believer's works are "burned down" he will not stand "blameless" before God. Thus, 1:8 was not intended to assert that a "blameless" state will be true of every Christian at the Judgment Seat of Christ. Paul speaks instead primarily about the spiritual status which he expects the Corinthian church to achieve corporately.

But even here caution must be exercised not to make the words say more than they actually do. If a counselor says to a troubled counselee, "God will strengthen you and see you through," this claim ought not to be viewed as a flat and unconditional prediction. Instead it is an expression of the counselor's conviction that God can be relied upon by the troubled individual who needs Him. Naturally he expects the counselee to appropriate God's help in the proper ways.

In 1 Corinthians 1:4–9 Paul begins his epistle on a positive note. He commends in the Corinthian church what there is to commend—there was a great deal to criticize!—and he expresses the expectation that "God will confirm you [that is, 'give you strength'] to the end, that you may be blameless in the day of our Lord Jesus Christ." But it is implicit in such a declaration that the Corinthians must *want* that strength and must appropriate it properly. Paul's main point is that God will furnish the needed help, because He is faithful (verse 9). Those who have elevated the statement of 1:8 to the level of a theological dictum about Christian perseverance have misconstrued the semantics of the text. They have also created false theology!

Philippians 1:6

As has often been pointed out, the Epistle to the Philippians is a "thank you" note. The Philippians have sent a monetary gift to Paul for which he is deeply grateful (4:10–19). Naturally at the very outset of the epistle he alludes to their material generosity. In 1:3–6 he writes:

> I thank God upon every remembrance of you, always in every prayer of mine making request for you all with joy,

for your fellowship in the gospel from the first day until
now, being confident of this very thing, that He who has
begun a good work in you will complete it until the day
of Jesus Christ.

It is natural to understand this passage in special reference to the
Philippians' recent generosity. This is implied rather plainly by
the Greek word "fellowship" which very often refers to material
"sharing" and can sometimes even mean "contribution" (see Rom.
15:26). Paul is assuring the Philippians that their "good work" of
sharing in the spread of the Gospel will be carried to full fruitage
by God. Its total effects (for example, in the winning of souls) will
only be manifest in the day of Jesus Christ.

Indeed, this very epistle can be seen as part of the fruit which
that "good work" produced, since the Philippians' gift occasioned
the letter. Whatever spiritual impact Paul's letter has had on the
Church down through the centuries (who can calculate it?) is
therefore part of the "interest" which has accrued on this simple
material investment in the cause of Christ. It may be suggested,
in fact, that every good work which we do has a potential for
usefulness that lies far beyond its original intent. God alone can
"perfect" our good works and give them their full impact—often
far beyond the lifetime of the one "in" whom the good work
begins. Only the day of Jesus Christ will disclose all that God does
with what we do for Him!

Philippians 1:6 is a lovely and thought-provoking utterance by
an appreciative Apostle. But to the issue of Christian perseverance
it has nothing to say at all.

Philippians 2:12, 13

More pertinent to the questions under discussion is Philippians
2:12, 13. There Paul writes:

Therefore, my beloved, as you have always obeyed, not
as in my presence only, but now much more in my ab-

sence, work out your own salvation with fear and trem-
bling; for it is God who works in you both to will and to
do for His good pleasure.

It is evident that if the "salvation" Paul speaks of here refers to
escape from hell, then obedient works are a *condition* for that.
Once again it would be unwarranted to import into the passage
the idea that such obedience is merely the evidence of true faith.
That concept has nothing whatsoever to support it in the text. It
can only amount to a semantic evasion of Paul's clear assertion
that this "salvation" must be "worked out." Whatever is involved
here, it is manifestly salvation by works!

It follows that Paul must be talking about something quite
different than the salvation he speaks of in Ephesians 2:8, 9 and
Titus 3:4–7. As a matter of fact he is. In only two other places in
this epistle does Paul employ the term "salvation." One of these
is in 1:19, 20 where he writes:

For I know that this will turn out for my salvation through
your prayer and the supply of the Spirit of Jesus Christ,
according to my earnest expectation and hope that in
nothing I shall be ashamed, but that with all boldness, as
always, so now also Christ will be magnified in my body,
whether by life or by death.

The first century reader is not likely to have had any problem
understanding this. The Greek word for "salvation" *(sōtēria)* was
a word meaning simply "deliverance." Like the English word
"deliverance" it could have wide application and was particularly
applicable to life-threatening situations. Paul now confronts a life-
threatening situation in which the outcome of his impending trial
cannot be predicted with absolute certainty.

His readers knew this, of course. When Paul writes, "I know
that this will turn out for my salvation," their first impression
would be that he anticipates release from his imprisonment. But

the remainder of his words show them that this is not what he has in mind. "For me," says Paul, "real 'deliverance' (or 'salvation') will consist of magnifying Christ whether I live or die. For this, I need your prayers and the help of God's Spirit."

In a very courageous way, therefore, Paul elevates his natural human concern with "deliverance" (or, "salvation") from trouble to the level of a spiritual concern that he will be "delivered" (or, "saved") from failing to honor God in whatever befalls him. In saying this, of course, he hopes to motivate his readers to similar objectives.

That, in fact, is exactly what he tries to do directly a little later in this chapter. In 1:27–30 he writes:

Only let your conduct be worthy of the gospel of Christ, so that whether I come and see you or am absent, I may hear of your affairs, that you stand fast in one spirit, with one mind striving together for the faith of the gospel, and not in any way terrified by your adversaries, which is to them a proof of perdition [or, "ruin," as it could be translated] but to you of salvation [or, "deliverance"], and that from God. For to you it has been given on behalf of Christ, not only to believe in Him, but also to suffer for His sake, having the same conflict which you saw in me and now hear is in me.

This admonition by the Apostle now applies to the readers the idea he had earlier expressed concerning himself. The Philippians too have sufferings just as he does. But they too can aspire to a "deliverance" (or, "salvation") in which Christ is magnified in them as well. Indeed, if they will stand unitedly for the Gospel and are not terrified by their adversaries, that will be the clearest proof that this "deliverance" (or, "salvation") is being realized in their lives. By contrast, their courage and fidelity foretells the ruin of their enemies, whether temporally or eternally.

Paul is aware, as are his readers, that there is a "deliverance" (or, "salvation") from hell which they have already attained by faith in Christ. But the "deliverance" (or, "salvation") he offers them here is over and above that which they already have. It is one that issues from sufferings. Hence, he can say, "For to you it has been granted . . . not only to believe in Him, but also to suffer for His sake." In other words, as there is salvation through faith, so there is one through sufferings. That too is being granted to you!

But *this* "salvation" (or, "deliverance") must be worked out! It is the product of obedience even under the most trying of circumstances. When Philippians 2:12, 13 is properly referred back to the Apostle's earlier references to "salvation," then its bearing becomes clear. Since this "salvation" consists essentially in honoring Christ by life or by death, it is necessarily inseparable from lives of obedience. In the words that immediately follow in 2:14–16, the quality of this kind of life is once more described. The Philippians are encouraged to be "children of God without fault in the midst of a crooked and perverse generation, among whom you shine as lights in the world" (2:15). Clearly such a result would be a signal triumph, a kind of spiritual "deliverance" or "salvation," in the midst of a hostile and dangerous earthly situation.

When the Greek translation of the Old Testament is taken into consideration, it can be safely said that by far the most common meaning of the word "salvation" in the Greek Bible is the one which refers to God's deliverance of His people from their trials and hardships. This significance is widespread in the Psalms above all. Among the references which might be cited are Psalm 3:8; 18:3, 35, 46, 50; 35:3; 37:39; 38:22; 44:4; etc. In all these places, and many more besides, the Septuagint translation employs the word *sōtēria* ("salvation"). First century Christians, therefore, were every bit as likely to construe a reference to "salvation" in this sense as they were to construe it in the sense of "escaping from hell."

New Testament expositors forget this fact *very* frequently. In place of careful consideration about the sense which the term "salvation" may have in any given context, there is a kind of expository "reflex action" that automatically equates the word with final salvation from hell. This uncritical treatment of many New Testament passages has led to almost boundless confusion at both the exegetical and doctrinal levels. Serious interpreters of the New Testament Scriptures must carefully avoid this kind of automatic response. They should seek rather to determine from the context the kind of "deliverance" in question. It may well be deliverance from death to life or from hell to heaven. But it may equally as well be a deliverance from trial, danger, suffering or temptation. The context—sometimes the larger context of the book itself (as in Romans and Hebrews)—must determine its exact meaning.

Furthermore, in the teaching of Jesus there emerges a distinctive note which is not really found in the Old Testament formulations about "salvation." While the old covenant saint thought instinctively of the preservation of his physical life, the new covenant person is taught to go beyond this conception. According to Jesus, a man can "save his life" even when he "loses" it (see Matt. 16:25 and parallels). This paradox suggests that even death itself cannot obliterate the value and worth of a life lived in discipleship to Christ. Such a life survives every calamity and issues in eternal reward and glory.

Paul is not far from such a thought in Philippians. To be truly "delivered" in suffering is not necessarily to survive it physically, but to glorify Christ through it. The same idea is present to the mind of the Apostle Peter in a famous passage on suffering found in 1 Peter 1:6–9. The expression in verse 9 which is rendered "the salvation of your souls" would be much better translated according to its normal Greek sense: "the salvation of your lives." Peter is describing the Messianic experience in which the believer partakes first of Christ's sufferings in order that he might subsequently share the glory to which those sufferings lead (1 Peter 1:10, 11). In this way the "life" is saved, even when paradoxically it is lost, because it issues in "praise, honor, and glory at the revelation of Jesus Christ" (1 Pet. 1:7).

Indeed it may be laid down that there is not a single place in the New Testament where the expression "to save the soul" ever means final salvation from hell. It cannot be shown that any native Greek speaker would ever have understood this expression in any other than the idiomatic way, that is, than as signifying "to save the life." The hardening of the idea of "saving the soul" into a fixed formulation about the final destiny of men may owe something to the unwanted influence of Greek philosophical discussions. But this contemporary use of the expression remains essentially foreign to the New Testament itself.

In Philippians Paul never uses the word "salvation" to refer to the question of heaven or hell. After all, both he and his readers *knew* where they were going! Their names were in the Book of Life (Phil. 4:3)!

Conclusion

Within the limited scope of this book it is obviously not possible to touch every single passage which at one time or another has been used to prove that Paul treated good works as an inevitable outcome of true regeneration. Paul simply did not hold such a view of works, though no writer insists more strongly than he that Christians ought to do them. Unfortunately, the Apostle has often not been credited with being truly consistent with his fundamental insistence that works have nothing to do with determining a Christian's basic relationship to God. That relationship, in Pauline thought, is founded on pure grace and nothing else.

Often Paul's statements are treated in a very one-dimensional way. Even though every epistle he wrote is addressed to those who have already come to saving faith, his assertions are too frequently taken as though he was constantly concerned about the eternal destiny of his readers. But there was no reason why he should have been, and his many direct affirmations that his audiences have experienced God's grace show that he was not. Such affirmations abound in the Pauline letters, and Ephesians 2 and Titus 3 are merely two of the most notable. Simple statements like, "For you were bought at a price; therefore glorify God in your body and in your spirit, which are God's" (1 Cor 6:20), show exactly what he thought about his readers' relationship to God. There is not even a single place in the Pauline letters where he expresses doubt that his audience is composed of true Christians.

Thus when the Apostle writes, "For as many as are led by the Spirit of God, these are the sons of God" (Rom. 8:14), he is not offering a "test" by which his readers may decide if they are saved or not! His readers possess a faith which "is spoken of throughout the entire world" (Rom. 1:8) and they enjoy "peace with God through our Lord Jesus Christ" as well as "access by faith into this grace in which we stand" (Rom. 5:1, 2; note the repeated use of "we"). That they could conceivably be unregenerate is the farthest thought from the Apostle's mind.

But for Paul the concept of being a "son of God" involved more than simply being regenerate. As he makes clear in Galatians 4:1-7, a "son" is one who has been granted "adult" status, in contrast to the "child" who is under "guardians and stewards" (Gal. 4:1, 2). This, of course, means that the Christian, as a "son," is free from the law. Thus the statement of Romans 8:14 is identical in force to that of Galatians 5:18: "But if you are led by the

Spirit, you are not under the law." That this is so is confirmed also by the reference to "the spirit of bondage" in Romans 8:15.

Consequently, both in Romans 8:14 and Galatians 5:18, Paul is talking about the way in which our freedom from the law is experientially realized. When the Spirit leads the life, there is no more legal bondage. The believer enters into the freedom of real "sonship" to God and that sonship becomes a reality in his day by day experience.

Nor should a "test" of regeneration be detected in a verse like Titus 1:16: "They profess that they know God, but in works they deny Him, being abominable, disobedient, and disqualified for every good work." It is superficial to take the word "deny" as though it meant nothing more than "is not a Christian." A little reflection will show that there are various ways in which a believer may "deny" God. He may do it *verbally*, as Peter did on the night of our Lord's arrest. But he may also do it *morally* by a lifestyle that contradicts the implications of the truth he professes. How easily this can be done even by a single act that clashes with our Christian profession, every honest Christian ought to be able to know out of his own experience.

Besides, the people Paul has in mind in Titus 1:16 are evidently the same as those of whom he says in verse 13: "Therefore rebuke them sharply, that they may be sound in the faith." The Greek word for "sound" means to be healthy. Hence, the persons he thinks of are not individuals who are not "in the faith" at all. Rather, they are people whom he regards as spiritually "sick" and who need a rebuke designed to restore them to good health. So far from showing that Christians cannot drift disastrously from the path of good works, Titus 1:16 shows the reverse!

Finally, an expression like "obedience to the faith" (Rom. 1:5; 16:26) has nothing to do with the works that follow salvation. The fact that it does not is widely recognized since the Greek expression is more literally rendered "the obedience of faith." In harmony with one well-known Greek usage of such expressions, the "obedience" in question is "faith" itself. Naturally, God demands that men place faith in His Son and is angry with them when they do not (John 3:36). Faith is an obedient response to the summons of the Gospel. But the man who exercises it is reaching out for the uncomplicated grace of God.

The Apostle Paul remains, therefore, the Apostle of divine grace. No doubt there were those who could twist his teachings into antinomian formulations (see Rom. 3:8). But this never deterred Paul from teaching the freeness of God's salvation nor did he neglect to inculcate a lifestyle that was truly responsive to this divine generosity. But the Apostle was also a realist and a pastor who knew only too well the failures to which Christians are prone. Yet he does not for that reason modify his conception of God's saving grace, but simply redoubles his efforts to stir up his fellow Christians to lives that honor their true calling (Eph. 4:1).

It may be safely said that no man in Christian history—with the exception of our Lord Himself—ever motivated believers more or threatened them less than did this great servant of Christ. Those who feel unable to inspire lives of obedience apart from questioning the salvation of those whom they seek to exhort, have much to learn from Paul!

CHAPTER

8

Faith and Water Baptism

The relationship of water baptism to the question of eternal salvation has been often discussed. It is well known that there are many churches where the rite of water baptism is regarded as an indispensable step in Christian conversion. A great deal of commentary literature on the New Testament has been authored by writers who are associated with such churches. It seems necessary to give at least brief consideration to this question here.

In the Gospel of John water baptism is never associated with the offer of eternal life. The only place that has often been alleged to do this is John 3:5 with its reference to being "born of water and the Spirit." But the deduction that "water" here must be a reference to water baptism is not well founded. If John really had believed that baptism was essential to the acquisition of eternal life, it is both astounding and inexplicable that he never says so directly. The passage can be adequately interpreted without making the equation "water" = "baptism."

Since the Greek word for "spirit" also meant "wind" it seems likely that the expression was originally intended to be understood as "born of water and wind" (see verse 8). In that case, "water" and "wind" are a dual metaphor intended to symbolize the quickening ministry of God's Spirit. Nicodemus should have been familiar with Old Testament texts which used these images of the Spirit's work (see Isaiah 44:3–5; Ezekiel 37:5–10). [This view of the text is defended by the present writer in some detail in an article, "Water and Spirit—John 3:5," *Bibliotheca Sacra*, vol. 135, no. 539, July-September, 1978, pages 206–220.] Suffice it to say here that there is no adequate reason to construe the utterance in connection with baptism. Indeed, the silence of the Fourth Gospel about the spiritual significance of this rite is almost deafening.

In the same way, the Apostle Paul can hardly be said to have viewed baptism as indispensable to his ministry in the Gospel. In fact, he actually writes, "For Christ did not send me to baptize, but to preach the gospel" (1 Cor. 1:17). It was apparently not his practice even to baptize his own converts (1 Cor. 1:13–16). At the very least, this does not sound like he thought no one could be eternally saved unless they were baptized! Outside of 1 Corinthians 1 (and 15:29) all the other references to Christian baptism in Paul can be adequately understood as references to baptism by the Holy Spirit. It was *this* baptism which was so vital to Pauline thought since it furnished the grounds on which the believer could be said to be *in* the body of Christ (see 1 Cor. 12:13).

It should be kept in mind that the key word in the Johannine doctrine of eternal salvation is "life," specifically "eternal life." For Paul the key word is "justification." Neither writer ever associates his basic idea with anything other than faith. For John, baptism plays no role in the acquisition of "life." For Paul it plays no role in "justification." But the further statement may be made that there is no New Testament writer who associates baptism with either of these issues. The importance of this cannot be overstated.

If this is properly kept in mind, a new light is cast on the kind of statement found in Acts 2:38. In that place, Luke reports the Apostle Peter as saying:

"Repent, and let every one of you be baptized in the name of Jesus Christ for the remission of sins; and you will receive the gift of the Holy Spirit."

This text seems clearly to say that the hearers must be baptized to get their sins forgiven and then, but only then, will they be given the gift of the Holy Spirit. An effort is sometimes made to avoid this conclusion by rendering the word "for" (Greek, *eis*) as "because of," but this procedure lacks adequate linguistic substantiation.

What the text does *not* say is how the hearers were "regenerated" and "justified." But the Pauline and Johannine answers to this question are the only Biblical ones that can be given: they were justified and regenerated by faith. *There is nothing in Acts 2:38 to contradict this!*

On the contrary, Peter concludes his address with the assertion that "God has made this Jesus, whom you have crucified, both Lord and Christ" (2:36). His hearers then reply, "Men and brethren, what shall we do?" (2:37). But such a reaction presumes their acceptance of Peter's claim that they have crucified the One who is Lord and Christ. If this is what they now believed, then they were already regenerate on Johannine terms, since John wrote: "Whoever believes that Jesus is the Christ is born of God" (1 John 5:1; cf. John 20:31).

It seems plain that in Peter's audience there are many who accept the claims of Christ. But they are enormously convicted of their guilt in the crucifixion and ask what they need to do now. Acts 2:38 is the answer. This verse could never have become a problem to interpreters as long as fundamental Pauline and Johannine declarations were kept in mind. Even the reference to the forgiveness of sins is not hard to comprehend when it is duly considered.

Justification by faith establishes a man's legal standing before his Judge. Forgiveness enables him to have communion with his God. Even on the level of everyday experience, forgiveness has nothing to do with the courts. But it has much to do with personal relationships. Men exclude from their fellowship those whom they refuse to forgive and are in turn excluded by those who will not forgive them.

It may be said then that when a man is justified he is given a righteousness which comes from God (Rom. 3:21–26). When he is regenerated, he is given the very life of God (John 1:12, 13). But forgiveness introduces him to fellowship with the One whose life and righteousness he has been granted through faith. Not surprisingly, therefore, even those who are both justified and regenerated are taught to seek forgiveness on a regular basis (Luke 11:4; 1 John 1:9). Justification and new birth are indefectible gifts. Communion is a conditional privilege.

The situation in Acts 2 is apparently exceptional. It is not repeated in the experience of Gentile converts (Acts 10:43–48). It is probably related to the special guilt of those who had been implicated in the crucifixion. But there is no actual conflict with fundamental Pauline and Johannine truth. Communion with God is withheld until baptism is undertaken, following which the gift of the Spirit is bestowed. But this latter gift was a new one, not bestowed before Pentecost (John 7:39). It is not to be confused with the experience of regeneration which has always been the fundamental requirement for entrance into God's Kingdom (John 3:3). At Pentecost, God gave the Spirit only to those who had entered into fellowship with Himself.

The experience just described was Paul's as well. Clearly Paul came to faith in the Lord Jesus Christ on the road to Damascus

(Acts 9:3-5; 22:6-8; 26:13-15). The blazing light in which he met his Savior has often been thought to inspire the imagery found in 2 Corinthians 4:6. Should the suggestion be made that Paul was not really converted on the Damascus road, this idea would be far-fetched in the extreme. Obviously, from that occasion onward, he was a believer in Jesus, whom he now calls Lord (Acts 22:10). But he was forgiven three days later! This is plainly affirmed by the words of Ananias in Acts 22:16 when he tells Saul, "Arise and be baptized, and wash away your sins, calling on the name of the Lord." Since his faith on the Damascus road had already brought him life and imputed righteousness, this additional step can only have introduced him into the dynamic experience of Spirit-led fellowship with God (see Acts 9:17-20). After three days of fasting and prayer (Acts 9:9, 11), he had found the answer to his question, "What shall I do, Lord?" (Acts 22:10). That answer, his Lord had told him, would be given to him in Damascus (Acts 9:6; 22:10).

That this type of experience is completely parallel to the situation of Acts 2:38—even down to the question, "What shall we do?"—is very obvious indeed. It is an experience in which baptism plays an important, but highly exceptional, role. Its terms are never repeated in the book of Acts anywhere on the Gentile mission fields. Neither are such terms presented anywhere in the epistles of the New Testament. They evidently belong to the historic record of God's dealings with that generation of Palestinians who had been exposed to, but had rejected, the ministries of both John the Baptist and Jesus Himself. (See the reference to "this perverse generation" in Acts 2:40.) In both the ministries of John and our Lord, baptism played a significant part (cf. John 4:1, 2), and its stipulation for people in this unique historical situation is entirely comprehensible.

It is along these lines, too, that the impartation of the gift of the Holy Spirit in Acts 19:1-7—after baptism!—is to be understood as well. The individuals involved were already believers as Paul's question to them makes plain: "Did you receive the Holy Spirit when you believed?" (19:2). But they were also evidently Palestinians since they had experienced John's baptism (19:3). In harmony with the conditions of Acts 2:38, Paul baptizes them and subsequently imparts to them the Holy Spirit (19:5, 6). But of non-Palestinians an experience like this is never predicated any-where in the New Testament. (Of course, the Samaritans of Acts 8:12-17 were Palestinians!)

Hence this is not normative Christian experience. Normative Christian experience takes the form set forth in the crucial story of the conversion of Cornelius in Acts 10. There forgiveness and the reception of the Spirit take place at the moment of faith (10:43, 44). Water baptism *follows* and in no way conditions these blessings (10:47, 48). The situations described in Acts 2, 8 and 19, as well as Paul's own, became a matter of instructive Biblical record. But by the time Paul wrote the Epistle to the Romans, it could be said that all Christians possessed the Spirit of God (Rom. 8:9; cf. 1 Cor. 12:13). The transitional features of the Christian message which Luke faithfully reports had ceased to be pertinent, as indeed they had never been on the Gentile fields.

This leads to a further important observation. In both the Lucan writings, and in Paul, the term "salvation," or "saved"—in ref-erence to converts to Christianity—is reserved for those who have received not only eternal life and justification, but also the gift of the Holy Spirit. Thus it is applied to the experience of Cornelius in direct connection with the gift of the Spirit (Acts 11:14-18). It is applied to the converts on the day of Pentecost only when they have been baptized and incorporated into the Church through the bestowal of the Spirit (Acts 2:47). It is the baptism of the Spirit, not new birth per se, that introduces men into the Body of Christ

(1 Cor. 12:13). Neither Luke nor Paul ever use the term "saved" of those not yet baptized with the Holy Spirit.

By contrast, John apparently can refer the term "saved" to those who have simply received eternal life. His use of the expression "saved" is rare, but the instances seem sufficient to prove the point just stated (John 3:17; 5:34; 10:9). But it must be carefully kept in mind that those who believed in Jesus during the course of His earthly life received only eternal life. The gift of the Spirit awaited the post-ascension situation. The Fourth Evangelist makes this point explicitly (John 7:39).

It follows from this that, in the Johannine sense, the converts of Acts 2 were "saved" *before* they were baptized. That is, they received eternal life the moment they believed in Jesus Christ. But in the Pauline and Lucan sense, they were not "saved" until *after* they were baptized, since only then did they receive the gift of the Spirit. It must be kept in mind, too, that all but the first century Palestinians received this "salvation" on the basis of faith alone. In Titus 3:4–7, the outpouring of the Holy Spirit is a prominent part of Paul's description of how God "saved" us.

If these distinctions are kept in mind, the significance of Mark 16:16 can be properly assessed. (The textual grounds for rejecting Mark 16:9–20 as not an authentic part of the original Gospel of Mark are exceedingly insufficient.) In Mark 16:16, Jesus states:

"He who believes and is baptized will be saved; but he who does not believe will be condemned."

Here it may be said that Jesus anticipates the Lucan and Pauline usage of the term "saved." That the bestowal of the Spirit, with His accompanying gifts, is in His mind is proved by verses 17, 18. Thus our Lord speaks of a "salvation" that involves *not only* eternal life, *but also* the gift of the Spirit.

Naturally His statement is a summary statement. It is designed to cover *all* the post-Pentecostal cases of "salvation." And exceptional as the situations of Acts 2, 8, and 19 are, they need to be comprehended in His declaration. Thus He affirms that *everyone* who takes the two steps specified will experience the "salvation" He is speaking of. Yet it has often been noticed that the condemnation in Mark 16:16 rests simply on the failure to believe. This is what we would expect. Eternal life is granted to faith alone (John 3:16; 5:24; etc.) and anyone who has it can never go to hell, whether they are baptized or not!

It is not possible here to fully analyze the famous passage in 1 Peter 3:18–22 in which there is a declaration that baptism "now saves us" (1 Pet. 3:21). Suffice it to say that the contextual emphasis on the Spirit and "spirits" (3:18, 19) points strongly to the conclusion that the Apostle has "Spirit baptism"—not water baptism—in mind. For the purposes of this discussion about the rite of baptism with water, 1 Peter 3:21 has nothing to contribute.

Finally, it should be said also that whenever an individual is baptized by the Holy Spirit and placed "in Christ," he receives at that moment a kind of "positional" forgiveness. This is described in Ephesians 1:7:

> **In Him** we have redemption through His blood, the forgiveness of sins, according to the riches of His grace [emphasis added].

Needless to say, like all else that pertains to our "position" in Christ, this forgiveness is perfect and permanent. But this in no way contradicts the fact that we also experience forgiveness continually at the level of our day to day experience.

Thus an unconverted sinner brings years of unforgiven sin to the moment of his conversion. Experientially, he acquires the forgiveness of all those past sins and commences his fellowship with God. But whenever he commits further sins, he must acknowledge them and seek God's forgiveness (Luke 11:4; 1 John 1:9). Nevertheless, as a man "in Christ" he has a position that is not altered by his daily experience of failure, and his relationship to God is never clouded, at this level of thought, by any earthly interruption in his communion with his Father.

The failure to distinguish our permanent experience of forgiveness "in Christ" from our daily experience of cleansing, has led to doctrinal confusion. It has actually led some to deny that a believer should ask for forgiveness for his sins, even though Christians are plainly enjoined to do so. After all, the Lord's prayer was given to *disciples*, not to unconverted sinners, and its petitions are to be made *daily* (Luke 11:1–4). The thought that a believer need never ask God's forgiveness for his sins is an aberration rightly rejected by the Church as a whole. But because a believer possesses eternal life, and is also "in Christ," his sins jeopardize only his fellowship with God day by day. They do not jeopardize his final salvation from hell.

At the level of everyday experience, repentance for our sins is as fitting for us as it was for the converts on the day of Pentecost (Acts 2:38). Only in our case, confession alone secures the forgiveness we need (1 John 1:9).

CHAPTER

9

Who Are The Heirs?

On the subject of heirship, the Apostle Paul has made a vital and instructive comment. His statement, found in Romans 8:16, 17, is as follows:

> The Spirit Himself bears witness with our Spirit that we are children of God, and if children, then heirs—heirs of God and joint heirs with Christ, if indeed we suffer with Him, that we may also be glorified together.

This declaration is often read as if fundamentally only one heirship were in view. However, with only a slight alteration of the English punctuation (which is equally permissible in the original Greek), Paul's words may be read thus:

> . . . and if children, then heirs—heirs of God, and joint heirs with Christ if indeed we suffer with Him, that we may also be glorified together.

Under this construction of the text, there are two forms of heirship. One of these is predicated on being children of God. The other is predicated on suffering with Christ. It may be pointed out at once that the thought of two kinds of heirship is extremely natural against the background of Old Testament custom. As is well-known, in a Jewish family all the sons shared equally in their father's inheritance, except for the eldest son who received a "double portion." That is, he inherited twice as much as the other sons.

Against this background, Paul may be understood as saying that *all* of God's children are heirs, simply because they are children. But those who suffer with Christ have a special "joint heirship" with Him. It is of the greatest significance in this connection that, later in this chapter, Christ is actually described as "the firstborn among many brethren" (8:29).

Naturally, all believers are God's heirs. In the eternal future they will most assuredly inherit all of the blessings which are unconditionally promised to them. Among these is an eternal glory (Rom. 8:30) which is inherent in the resurrection itself. Hence Paul can say, "The body is sown in corruption, it is raised in incorruption. It is sown in dishonor, it is raised in glory. It is sown in weakness, it is raised in power" (1 Cor. 15:42, 43). Elsewhere he writes that "we also eagerly wait for the Savior, the Lord Jesus Christ, who will transform our lowly body that it may be conformed to His glorious body" (Phil. 3:20, 21).

Needless to say, participation in the resurrection is unconditionally guaranteed to every believer on the basis of his faith in Christ alone. Jesus' own declaration on this point is definitive:

> "For I came down from heaven, not to do My own will, but the will of Him who sent Me. And this is the will of the Father who sent Me, that of all He has given Me I should lose nothing, but should raise it up at the last day. And this is the will of Him who sent Me, that everyone who sees the Son and believes in Him may have ever-

lasting life; and I will raise him up at the last day" (John
6:38–40).

Few passages are more decisive concerning the eternal security
of the believer in Christ. The Lord Jesus Christ has never lost, nor
will he ever lose, anyone who has belonged to Him through faith.
But equally, though the word "inheritance" is not used here, such
words seal the heirship of every Christian. A share in the glorious
immortality of the future world is assured to him, because Jesus
has promised to "raise him up at the last day."

But in Romans 8:17, Paul speaks also of a "co-heirship" that
results in "co-glory." This contrast is a bit easier to see in Greek
than it is in English. Thus Paul juxtaposes in the Greek text two
words for "heir," one of which is the simple word for this and the
other a compound word roughly equal to our word "co-heir."
Similarly, compound words express the thought of "co-suffering"
and "co-glorification." But as Paul's words make clear, such an
heirship is dependent on something more than saving faith. Indeed, it is an heirship that is contingent on our experience of
suffering with Christ.

A similar thought recurs in Paul in 2 Timothy 2:12. There the
Apostle writes, "If we endure, we shall also reign with Him."
Here again we meet the thought of suffering, since the Greek
verb "endure" refers primarily to the endurance of hardships and
trials. Moreover, the verb rendered "reign with Him" is another
compound word such as we meet in Romans 8:17. The idea is:
"If we endure [suffering], we shall co-reign" (the words "with
Him" are implied by the compound verb).

Putting Romans 8:17 together with 2 Timothy 2:12, it is natural
to conclude that to be "co-glorified" with Christ involves "co-
reigning" with Him. In other words, the glory of co-heirship is
more than merely participating in the glorious future world. It is
to share the portion of the Firstborn and to REIGN there! With

so glorious a prospect in view, no wonder Paul aspired to know Christ in "the fellowship of His sufferings" (Phil. 3:10)!

The connection between fidelity to Christ and the privilege of sharing the authority of His Kingdom appears already in the teaching of Jesus Himself. Its most striking expression is found in the famous parable of the minas in Luke 19:11–27. The parable begins with a reference to the inter-advent period in which we live today as we wait for the Kingdom of God. Jesus introduces the story with these words:

> "A certain nobleman went into a far country to receive for himself a kingdom and to return. And he called his ten servants, delivered to them ten minas, and said to them, 'Do business till I come.'" (Lk. 19:12,13).

It is easy to see how this relates to contemporary Christian experience. The minas (a mina was a unit of money) represent the potential for useful service to Christ with which every believer is intrusted. His marching orders are: "Do business till I come."

According to the story which Jesus told, when the nobleman returned he called each of his servants to account. This clearly suggests the Judgment Seat of Christ (Rom. 14:10–12; 2 Cor. 5:9, 10; 1 Cor. 3:11–15; 4:5). But the outcome of the assessment, as the parable unfolds it, is varying degrees of authority in the Kingdom based on the measure of each servant's faithfulness and productivity. Thus one servant receives authority over ten cities (19:17), another over five (19:19).

Both, however, are sharply distinguished from the unproductive servant, who is given no cities to rule and is even deprived of his mina (19:22–24). He thus bears an unmistakable resemblance to a Christian whose works are "burned down" and who "will be saved, yet so as through fire" (1 Cor. 3:15). He had a job to do but he failed to do it. He is therefore stripped of further responsibility. His mina is taken away!

As has been insisted upon in the previous chapters, the belief that every Christian will live a basically successful life until the end is an illusion. It is not supported by the instruction and warnings of the New Testament. There is a sense in which all Christians are heirs of God. But they are not heirs to an equal degree. Their fidelity to the service of Christ, with all its attendant hardships and sufferings, will be the guage by which that heirship will be measured out to them. Not to teach this simple truth is to deprive believers of one of the most powerful motivations to endurance which the Scriptures contain.

It is not surprising that those who do not perceive this aspect of New Testament revelation have impoverished their ability to motivate both themselves and other believers. Tragically, they often fall back on the technique of questioning the salvation of those whose lives seem not to meet Biblical standards. But in the process they undermine the grounds for a believer's assurance and take part—however unwittingly—in the siege of the Gospel.

Paul did not do this, even though he has sometimes been read as if he did. In writing to the Corinthian church he is exasperated that they engage in lawsuits against one another. Of course, he does not question the salvation of those who do this. Instead he says,

> But brother goes to law against brother, and that before unbelievers! (1 Cor. 6:6)

The enormity of this, from Paul's point of view, is that Christians carry Christians to court where unsaved people preside! He deplores this emphatically.

His critique of such conduct continues:

> Now therefore it is already an utter failure for you that you go to law with one another. Why do you not rather accept wrong? Why do you not rather let yourselves be

> defrauded? No, you yourselves do wrong and defraud,
> and you do these things to your brethren! (1 Cor. 6:7, 8)

It is precisely at this point that the Apostle turns to the theme of heirship, for he goes on to say:

> Do you not know that the unrighteous will not inherit the
> kingdom of God? Do not be deceived. Neither fornicators,
> nor idolators, nor adulterers, nor effeminate homosex-
> uals, nor sodomites, nor thieves, nor covetous, nor drunk-
> ards, nor revilers, nor extortioners will inherit the kingdom
> of God (1 Cor. 6:9, 10).

It is as plain as it can possibly be that the Apostle intends these words as a warning against the kind of conduct he has been describing in the Corinthian Christians. This is made doubly obvious by the opening assertion that "the *unrighteous* will not inherit the kingdom of God" since he has just charged them with being unrighteous. This fact is even plainer in Greek than in English since the word translated "you do wrong" in verse 8 is the Greek verb *adikeite,* and the word for "unrighteous" in verse 9 is its cognate, *adikoi.*

What Paul is saying therefore is that they are engaged in the very kind of conduct that makes it impossible to inherit the Kingdom of God. Persistence in this type of behavior will obviously disqualify them from this kind of heirship. No other deduction about his meaning can possibly be fair to the text.

But does he thereby call their salvation into question? That is precisely what he does NOT do! Instead he writes:

> And such were some of you. But you were washed, but
> you were sanctified, but you were justified in the name
> of the Lord Jesus and by the Spirit of our God (1 Cor.
> 6:11).

So far from suggesting to them that perhaps they are not Christians after all, he appeals to the fact that they are!

Obviously, too, his list of vices with its heavy stress on immorality is a part of his larger unhappiness with the conduct of the Corinthian Christians (see 1 Cor. 5:1–13; 6:12–20). But always he appeals to the certitude that they are Christians, not to the possibility that they are not. So he can say as well:

Do you not know that your bodies are the members of Christ? Shall I then take the members of Christ and make them members of a harlot? Certainly not! (1 Cor. 6:15)

And he ends the chapter with the appeal:

Or do you not know that your body is the temple of the Holy Spirit who is in you, whom you have from God, and you are not your own? For you were bought at a price; therefore glorify God in your body and in your spirit, which are God's (6:19, 20).

The Apostle's whole argument for the moral rectitude of his hearers is predicated on the fact that they are indeed truly God's property. They ought to act like what they are!

The widespread notion that Paul actually doubted—or, could doubt—the salvation of his readers on the basis of their behavior, is so far from his real perspective that it is virtually incomprehensible how that deduction could ever be drawn. Such an approach to his assertions here about heirship is so hopelessly confused that it manages to miss his point entirely and to derive from these assertions an outlook that was totally alien to Paul's mind!

In speaking of heirship in 1 Corinthians 6:9, 10, the Apostle did not threaten his readers with the loss of eternal salvation. He did not even raise a question about their salvation. But he warned them plainly that if they did not correct their unrighteous behavior, they confronted a serious consequence. They would not inherit the Kingdom of God.

Many have assumed, without much thought, that to "inherit" the Kingdom must be the same as entering it. But why should such an equation be made? Even in everyday speech there is a difference between saying, for example, "you will *live* in that house" and "you will *inherit* it." If a wealthy man tells me that I will inherit his house, has he told me nothing more than that I shall inhabit it someday? Obviously, he has told me more that that! He has told me that I will *own* that house. And the more wealthy the man is, and the larger his house is, the more significant that promise becomes. It is extremely careless not to give deeper thought to a significant concept like "inheriting" the Kingdom of God.

It should certainly be clear upon reflection that the Kingdom does not really belong to those who are only citizens there. Citizens are *subjects* of a Kingdom, not its owners! The Kingdom belongs to the King who wields authority there. It can only belong to others if He deigns to *share* His authority with them. To put it plainly, the Kingdom of God can belong only to those who are "co-heirs" with Jesus Christ and who "co-reign" with Him.

But for this privilege, perseverance in holiness is an indispensable condition. That point is plainly stated in Revelation 2:26, 27:

> "And he who overcomes and keeps My works until the end, to him I will give power over the nations—'And he shall rule them with a rod of iron; as the vessels of a potter they shall be broken to pieces'—as I also received from My Father."

In a quite similar vein, we read also in Revelation 3:21:

> "To him who overcomes I will grant to sit with Me on My throne, as I also overcame and sat down with My Father on His throne."

It is clear that spiritual victory—and keeping Christ's works until the end—are essential if one wishes to sit with Him on His throne! But could there be any greater challenge to such victory than so splendid an outcome?

In 1 Corinthians 6:9–11, Paul's point is simple and direct. Unrighteous people of the type he describes can never be co-heirs with Jesus Christ. They can never "inherit" the Kingdom of God. And that is exactly what some of the Corinthians *formerly were.* But now the slate has been wiped clean by the grace of God. "You were washed," "you were sanctified," "you were justified"! So don't become those things again and forfeit the inheritance that otherwise can be yours!

Those who find in Paul's words some kind of "test" of a man's salvation might almost be suspected of hardly having read the text!

Needless to say, the similar Pauline passage found in Galatians 5:21 is to be interpreted in exactly the same way. Here too the assertion about "inheriting" the Kingdom of God occurs in the heart of an exhortation that warns believers against the danger of fulfilling "the lust of the flesh" (Gal. 5:16–26). Evidently the Apostle used this truth as a powerful motivational technique for his Christian brethren. It goes without saying, so should we!

Indeed, the Scriptures open up to the faithful believer a marvelous and varied vista of the future. The promises to the "overcomers" in Revelation 2 and 3 are a significant part of this vista. Here we meet, as a proferred reward, the mysterious "tree of life, which is in the midst of the Paradise of God" (Rev. 2:7). Naturally, a person who has Christ within him will not need a physical tree, however wonderful, to sustain the spiritual life within him. But that such a tree might offer some kind of superlative experiential enrichment is an obvious—and tantalizing— conception. Whatever the tree of life has to offer those who are granted the right to partake of it, this must be supremely worth striving for!

It seems evident that in treading the terrain set before us in these promises to the "overcomers," we come close to realities impossible to describe precisely to men still in their earthbound flesh. Paul had once been exposed to "inexpressible words" which he was not allowed to repeat (2 Cor. 12:4). The vagueness surrounding the promise of the tree of life is an example of the deliberate inexplicitness of the rewards which are mentioned. Almost all of the other promises have something of the same undefined, but numinous, character.

Two of them at least seem to employ a well-known figure of speech called litotes. In litotes an affirmative idea is expressed through the negation of its opposite. Vagueness is often the intended result of this kind of speech. Thus I may say, "If you do me this favor, I will not forget you." "I will not forget you" is a litotes for something like, "I will repay you well."

The two promises to "overcomers" which can most readily be interpreted as involving a litotes are these:

He who overcomes shall not be hurt by the second death (Rev. 2:11).

He who overcomes shall be clothed in white garments, and **I will not blot out his name from the Book of Life;** but I will confess his name before My Father and before His angels (Rev. 3:5; emphasis added).

Every Christian who remembers the direct teaching of the Gospel of John will know that the Apostle John himself did not understand these promises as threatening the failing Christian with "the second death" or with the erasure of his name from "the Book of Life." And again, there is absolutely nothing in these letters to suggest that all Christians are "overcomers." If Revelation 2 and 3 are read thoughtfully, it will be found that they suggest the reverse!

Of course, when a believer exercises faith in Christ, he *does* overcome the world in that sense (1 John 5:4, 5). The world system is intrinsically hostile to that kind of faith and is satanically blinded to the truth (2 Cor. 4:3, 4). The very act of faith at the moment of regeneration—and, indeed, every subsequent act of faith—is a signal victory over the world. But this is a long way from saying that all Christians live ultimately victorious lives. In fact, that is something the New Testament does NOT say!

The promises of Revelation 2:11 and 3:5 are best understood as litotes. John and all his intelligent Christian readers knew that a believer would never experience the second death. But the promise of 2:11 claims that this death will not even do him any *damage*. The Greek verb rendered "hurt" might easily be translated "injured." The Smyrnan Christians who are "faithful until death" (2:10) will not even be *injured* by it. By litotes this intimates a superlative triumph over the second death. But since the second death is actual banishment from the presence and life of God (Rev. 20:14, 15), the litotes also intimates a splendid experience of the divine life and presence.

The litotes in 3:5 is equally easy to understand. Again John and his readers know that no Christian can have his name blotted out of the Book of Life. They also know that there is great honor in having one's name inscribed there (see Luke 10:20). The litotes here is something like saying, "Your honored name will never be erased." But this suggests, "Your name will be glorious forever," or something similar. The fact that honor is the basic issue in this particular promise is clearly shown by the other elements of the promise. Special white garments (a mark of dignity in ancient thought) are to be granted the "overcomer" and his enduringly honored name is to be openly acknowledged before God and the holy angels.

Finally, it should be noted that both promises are especially suited to the particular trials which the Christians in each church must confront and overcome. At Smyrna there was persecution and the possibility of death (2:10), but fidelity even unto death is to be met with a suitable reward: a superlative triumph over the second death. At Sardis the problem to be conquered was that of an empty "name" (3:1). The reward is fitting: a name whose honor can never be expunged.

But those who allege that fidelity even to martyrdom, and the capacity to rise above the spiritual lethargy around us, are in fact inevitable consequences of simply being a true Christian, are looking at life from an ivory tower that is totally divorced from the down-to-earth realism of the New Testament writers. If we refuse to face the possibility of failure, we in fact prepare the way for that failure.

"Therefore let him who thinks he stands take heed lest he fall" (1 Cor. 10:12).

The price of spiritual victory is high. Let no one be under any delusion about that. But the price is well worth paying. Every sacrifice will be more than amply rewarded!

CHAPTER

10

Grace Triumphant

Perhaps it would be well to restate the thesis of this book as clearly as possible. Some of the related consequences of this thesis can also be specified by way of summation.

Basically it is maintained that the New Testament Gospel offers the assurance of eternal life to all who will accept that life by faith in Christ. The assurance of the believer rests squarely on the direct promises in which this offer is made, and on nothing else.

It follows from this that the assertion that a believer must find his assurance in his works, is a grave and fundamental theological error. It is an error that goes right to the heart of the nature of the Gospel proclamation. It seriously distorts that proclamation and creates in its place a new kind of message that would have been unrecognizable to the New Testament writers.

This is a serious charge. But it is made thoughtfully and with much grief that it is necessary to make it at all.

Preachers and theologians cannot have it both ways. Either a man can be perfectly sure that he is born again and going to heaven at the moment he trusts Christ, or he cannot. If works must verify a man's faith, then he cannot. It can even be argued that he can never be sure until he meets God. But this is not what the New Testament teaches. It is therefore a falsehood and subversive of Biblical truth.

Let it be said clearly that the point of this book is NOT to argue that Christians should not take sin seriously. Of course they should. In fact they should cast themselves on the strength and power of God to avoid it. And victory in their lives, along with rich fellowship with the Father and the Son, is marvelously available to all who do so. So this book is not written to justify the sin and failure that so often occur in the Christian Church. There is an attempt here to face that failure honestly, just as the New Testament writers do. But there is no attempt to excuse it.

This book is about the Gospel. And it is also about a Satanic siege of the Gospel in which the simplicity, clarity and freeness of the Gospel message have come under assault. It is an effort to focus the Church on the issues that are at stake in this attack. It is the prayer of the writer that many will be aroused to stand firmly for the true grace of God.

Grim as the battle is, however, its outcome is not in doubt. Grace will be triumphant. No matter how much confusion the Enemy of souls is able to inject into professing Christendom, there will always be those who understand and proclaim God's free gift of eternal life. The Bible is clear on this point and God's message has never lacked messengers.

But grace will be triumphant in another way as well. Someday the failures now so painfully evident among those who trust Christ will be forever gone. Everyone who has ever accepted God's gracious salvation will one day be conformed to the image of His Son (Romans 8:29) and will enter the eternal world totally free from the least trace of sin. No doubt not all of them will have attained to "co-heirship" with Jesus Christ, but all of them will be among history's immortals!

It is one measure of the triumph of God's grace that the Apostle John can describe the eternal state with these words:

> But the cowardly and unbelieving and abominable and murderers and sexually immoral and sorcerers and idolators and all liars shall have their part in the lake which burns with fire and brimstone, which is the second death (Rev. 21:8).

This is not, of course, salvation by works after all! It is rather a declaration that in the new heavens and the new earth (cf. Rev. 21:1), there are no more cowards, no more idolators, no more liars—except those who have been consigned to the lake of fire!

But what about born again Christians who have done these things? To be specific, what about wise Solomon who ended his life with defection from his God and with idolatry (1 Kings 11:1–10)! The answer is that they will all be in the presence of God as citizens of the eternal world. And whatever their failures on earth may have been, these are gone. If they had been liars, they are liars no more. If idolators, they are idolators no more. For now they are immortal and sinless. They are conformed to the image of God's Son.

How did they come to this place? By the grace of God. For even when God's people fail Him, He does not fail them. He always keeps His Word. In that sense, too, grace will be triumphant!

No wonder that it is with direct reference to God's faithfulness that the great Apostle of grace declares: "Indeed, let God be true but every man a liar" (Rom. 3:4)! And again, in 2 Timothy 2:13, he wrote:

> If we are faithless, He remains faithful; He cannot deny Himself.

EPILOGUE

When Jimmy got home from work that night, he got out his Bible and began to read the Gospel of John.

Pretty soon he had read verses like John 1:12; 3:16; 4:10; and 5:24. As he did so his assurance and joy began to return.

"I sure don't know where Bill is coming from," he said to himself, "but I know what these verses are saying. I know I have believed, so I know I have everlasting life!"

With the return of joy came a renewed desire to please God, not to prove he was saved, but out of gratitude for God's goodness.

A casualty in the siege of the Gospel? Yes, for a while. But it was only a surface wound. And the curative powers of God's Word are tremendous.

What Jimmy needs now is a church that preaches a clear Gospel and that expounds God's truth faithfully and well.

Meanwhile, he really *is* saved and God's faithfulness will not fail him.

The prognosis is good. Jimmy will be all right!